Easy Money

A "Bankspeak" Primer for Small Business

By Leslie D. Marion

4th Floor Press

©2020 Leslie D. Marion

All rights reserved. No part of this publication may be reproduced in any form or by any means without the express prior written consent of the publisher and/or author, other than short excerpts (300 words or less) for reviews.

THE AUTHOR HAS MADE EVERY EFFORT TO ENSURE THAT THE INFORMATION IN THIS BOOK IS CORRECT AND ACCURATE. WE DO NOT ASSUME AND HEREBY DISCLAIM ANY LIABILITY TO ANY PARTY FOR ANY LOSS, DAMAGE, OR DISRUPTION CAUSED BY THE INFORMATION CONTAINED HERE. SOME OF THE NAMES OF INDIVIDUALS HAVE BEEN CHANGED TO PRESERVE THEIR PRIVACY.

ISBN 978-1-7771032-2-4
eISBN 978-1-7771032-1-7
eISBN 978-1-777-1032-0-0

4th Floor Press, Inc.
www.4thfloorpress.com
1st Printing 2020
Printed in Canada
Cover Image by Andrew Foley

Acknowledgements

I wouldn't be writing this book without my partner Jack Lawson. He decided to go back to school to get his Masters in Fine Arts—Creative Non-Fiction in 2016 and in the process I decided he couldn't have all the fun. I joined him and that's where this book started. He edited many versions before it was published. He pushed me to help people understand.

I owe to Niel (and Liz his partner) as without them this would simply be a how-to without concrete results. He and Liz (she asked as I sent it to him—that's the kind of person she is?) read the manuscript and were onside.

My friend Corey Keith and his wife Wendy let me (and you!) understand what the difference is between *angel investors* and *Venture capital*. Fred was amazing because he helped me understand what angels do!

My mom, Rae (or, as I refer to her, Tubby Al), read the book before she passed on—and was delighted. My dad, George, was very pleased I was writing it but he didn't see the finished product. My brother, Jack, sent an email that said, "My sister the author. Way to go!"

Wayne Boss and my sister-in-law Terri Theodore read the final version. Their input was invaluable (and made it more understandable!).

My friend Marlene and her son Andrew Foley designed the cover. I didn't know what I wanted except caricatures of a blue-collar and white-collar worker so they did an amazing job! Her husband Joe took the pictures for the head-shot.

Of course, I owe accolades to those that helped me learn throughout my career—both mentors and clients. Without them, I would never have learned. Don Sedgewick, Kimberly Pittaway, Tim Falconer, Jane Hamilton Silcott, Harry K. Thurston, Stephen Kimber, and Dean Jobb were the faculty at King's College School of Journalism who worked tirelessly with me over the course of two years. Kim still helps out.

Cheers—and I hope this helps you!

CONTENTS

Acknowledgements	iii
Introduction	1
Chapter 1: Walk Before You Run to Your Banker	10
Chapter 2: Where Do You Go to Get Money and How Do You Get There?	33
Chapter 3: Why Cash is King!	54
Chapter 4: The Five "Cs" of Credit and Loan Pricing	81
Chapter 5: What Options Are There for Financing and What Are You Agreeing To?	106
Chapter 6: Non-Conventional Sources of Financing and What They Mean	138
Chapter 7: Niel and Valley Floors Inc.— A Case Study	157
Glossary	172
ABOUT THE AUTHOR	197

Introduction

My first job as an account manager was in the Kelowna Main Branch and my first loan was to a woman who wanted to open a cellulite clinic. I loaned her $3,000 as an *overdraft* and when she couldn't afford to make the first interest payment, the bank had to write the loan off. My fellow account managers, who were all male, presented me with a small trophy with an inscription—The Kinky Account of the Week Award—that I still have on my bookcase. That was in August 1979. That was a shocking eye-opener for me. I guess that is when I learned that the first "C" of credit, *character*, was so important. I didn't believe for a minute that she couldn't or wouldn't pay me back. I don't recall even doing a *credit bureau* check on her. I was not the least objective and simply lent her money because she wanted it.

In the forty-plus years since then, I've learned that access to money can be easier with communication and a little insight into what lenders want from you to help your business succeed. I'll provide anecdotes and interviews with small business owners, including *entrepreneurs*, to illustrate the relationship they had with their bankers—what worked, what didn't, and what both could have done differently.

Before I was posted to my first job as an account manager, one of the branches needed a manager for vacation relief. I was finished my training and waiting to be placed so I was available. It didn't seem to matter that I knew nothing about running a branch as my education and training were focussed on finance and analyzing how a loan would be repaid. In the first week, one of the most important clients of the branch needed a loan so I asked him every question I could think of and told him I would get back to him within a few days. I shut my door and picked up the phone and called Barry who was in the loan approval department. Barry walked me through how to present the application and within days the loan was approved and we had a happy customer. That was then, though, and things have changed.

It is not surprising that things are done differently now than they were then. I have been involved in lending since 1979 and have over forty years of experience in helping businesses succeed. Until 1999, I was employed by a bank and did stints as both a marketer and credit approver—in bank terminology an account manager and a risk manager so I understand what it takes to get a bank to lend money for a business. I was instrumental in providing loans to businesses that ranged from small *overdrafts* to structuring, recommending and having approved a successful U.S. $500 million facility. Since 1999, I have focused on developing and teaching courses on understanding small businesses and how to lend to them.

My partner and I are also small business owners. I understand the borrower side of ***Easy Money*** as I am an *entrepreneur*. Jack started his company in 1988 and in 1999, after twenty years, I left the bank and joined his company. From 1993 to 1998, while I was still with the bank, we ran a bulk and natural food store in the heart of the Rocky Mountains. I was a great "Deli lady" on the weekends and accountant and banker during the week, but after five years we had learned more than enough about retailing and sold the store.

As small business owners, we are part of a majority of businesses in both Canada and the U.S. According to Statistics Canada and the U.S. Census Bureau, small businesses represent over ninety percent of all businesses in the U.S. and that increases to ninety-five percent in Canada. That's over six million enterprises and the number is growing every year. Almost all of them need financing at some point and some need it as long as they operate. Lending to small business is big business in both countries.

Providing support to these small enterprises is critical to our employment figures as well. In Canada, they represent seventy percent of all jobs and in the U.S. about fifty percent. But, small businesses generally cannot succeed without some financial assistance, which often is a bank loan, and most are somewhat timid when it comes to meeting and sharing information with their banker. Both sides need to understand what information is required and how to provide it, and both can win if the relationship becomes a partnership, rather than a power trip. ***Easy Money*** will concentrate on what concerns the banks and how a borrower can best help a banker provide what they need. For the borrower, knowledge is power. It is up to the business owner to help develop the sales pitch.

Easy Money is the guide that will help you understand how to get the money you need to make your business successful. It will focus on lending to small and medium-sized businesses and explore their owners' successes and failures through case studies and anecdotes.

The terms "small business owner" and "*entrepreneur*" are often used interchangeably. I describe an *entrepreneur* as "someone who tries something and if it doesn't work just picks himself up, dusts himself off and tries something else." While most *entrepreneur*s are small business owners, not all small business owners are *entrepreneurs*. True *entrepreneurs* make up a small proportion of small business owners—likely less than ten percent. There is a striking difference between individuals who go into business because they are good at something and those who thrive on innovation, new ideas, and are prepared to take more risk. Neither is better, but both borrowers and lenders need to understand which the customer is because motivations and expectations will be different. I have met both over the years and will provide some insight into each.

A lot has changed since I started banking. At that time, we did not have the technology to figure out which customers made the most money. In a training course in the early 1980s, we were told if banks could ever figure out and get rid of the accounts that were costing us money, "the unprofitable tail," we would free up a lot of our time and make a lot more money. That has happened and bankers spend more time with profitable clients. If a business doesn't provide enough revenue to the bank, or at least have a lot of potential, the banker will not spend much time with it. That's more the case with large banks. Some smaller regional or member-owned lenders don't differentiate.

The folks who are the bank's face to borrowers are account managers, or relationship managers, and are the sales force. They are typically managed by sales managers. The folks that sell the loans and those who decide whether you can have one are usually not the same people. The sales manager has to tell your story to someone else who will also assess the business's ability to pay back the loan and then recommend it to someone else to get it approved. The problem is that a lot of the sales force doesn't know what makes a good loan. Salespeople selling a product they don't understand to customers who need guidance is the cause of much of the dissatisfaction and distrust that small businesses have with financial institutions today.

Business owners use loans as part of their day to day business and banks consider loans to be a product with a promise to repay. For bankers, selling products is what pays the bills and competition has increased a lot. In most sales, the seller does not want to get the product back. Lending is more complicated—banks expect to get their product (the money) back. Money is rented to you under terms and *conditions* for a fee until you return it. It is up to the banker, with your help, to determine whether you will be able to pay them back.

Most banks typically look at the risk rating of a potential borrower based on the five *Cs of credit*:

- **Character**—who you are and your reputation;
- **Capacity**—can the loans be repaid from cash generated by the business;
- **Collateral**—if the business is not successful, is there a second way out and will the liquidation of any *security* repay the loans;
- **Conditions**—the terms of the transaction that protect the borrower and the lender if unexpected events occur;

- **Capital**—is there sufficient *equity* in the company to provide a buffer if things do not turn out as planned.

As I discovered early in my career, the most important C is *character*. Banks need to know who they are lending to. That is the first hurdle. If there's no trust between them, the relationship generally ends badly. Most banks don't lend more money to someone who has not paid them back in the past. I had a call from an account manager with a question about a guy whose business had failed because the economy had gone into the tank and he couldn't pay back his loans. He was a shareholder in a new company that wanted loans. My question was simple. How did he react when things went bad in the past? Did he walk in and say "you have a problem" or was it "we have a problem and I'll do what I can to help." Fortunately, he was prepared to help and he was able to pay back some of the loans. Because of his attitude, the bank helped his new business.

Bankers were told in the early days not to give advice as that was considered an invitation for a lawsuit. Now customers should expect it and will likely be hooked up with someone who knows the industry and can help them navigate. In return, customers are expected to share what they know. That's how bankers learn and help customers.

The relationship between bankers and small businesses has changed dramatically. Until recently, business owners went to the bank to meet with bankers. Historically, these bankers had chairs that were higher than clients to make sure they looked down on them and had a feeling of a sense of power. Understandably, most clients felt intimidated. Bankers now visit clients. They want to see the business and understand how it operates. They learn so much about the *character* of borrowers by seeing them interact in their own business, both with customers and employees.

For some reason, borrowers often share only the good news with their banker but they also need to share the bad news. Bankers hate surprises and if you share the bumps in the road with them, they can often help. We lent half of what a restaurant designer needed to build a new restaurant and he never offered that he did not have the other half (nor did the banker ask him). We had to ask him to find a new bank because he was not living up to his commitment to us and was also breaking the law. Had he advised us in the beginning, we may have found a different solution.

The trust that makes the relationship work is built on the same foundations of honesty and integrity that is the basis of any partnership and the responsibility is a joint one. I have found that long-term relationships often endure because the borrower remembers the first interaction and it was positive. On the reverse side, borrowers who do not think they were treated well when they started their business will often move to a different bank when the first opportunity arises. Nobody wins in that case, except the new banker.

There are lots of places to get money and I talk about what they are and how and when you might use each one. Family, friends, and your own resources are a major source, especially for a start-up company. There are also other *equity* investors, lenders and *grants*. Everyone who gives you money wants to know you have "skin in the game" so it is not as easy to walk away. As lenders, banks don't get paid a lot and don't get to share in the *profits* when you make a lot of money like an investor or some other lenders do. In the event the business doesn't work, you will be paid last. Others, like your suppliers, hope they will be paid as well. The more cash you have in the company, the more likely others will get paid back.

I have included a glossary in the back of this book and have printed in italics those terms throughout to save you time. I have changed the names of some of the individuals to preserve their privacy.

Chapter 1

Walk Before You Run to Your Banker

What you need to consider before you go into business and why Marie didn't

In early 2014, we knew we had to either renovate the condominium we had lived in for thirty years or move. We had to replace cupboards, floors, bathrooms, and remove a wall just to name a few of the changes. We couldn't replace the location, view or amenities (like two wood-burning fireplaces and two large decks) so renovation it would be. We found our general contractor, Keith, at the Renovation Show in Calgary. He was ex-military and had been in the business for just over a year. His strength was clearly in his vision and that likely came about because he was also a photographer. As examples, he proposed shiny white cupboards throughout, including the floor to ceiling bookcases where we would have chosen dark wood, and suggested cork instead of hardwood. The best advice he probably gave us was to hire an interior decorator with an eye for detail to do the legwork and help us pick out things like tile and fixtures. We hired

Carol and she was worth every penny.

Keith was a one-man show, although his girlfriend and thirteen-year-old daughter helped him out on occasion. We found out during the summer that working was clearly not his passion—he took four day weekends even when we had no cupboards as he wanted to spend the time on his sailboat. Unfortunately, the renovation put such a strain on him he disappeared before finishing the job. One of Keith's sub-trades was Niel, a flooring guy, who was absolutely amazing. He even came back the next year and spent two days of his own time and on his own dime to make things right for us. Niel stood behind his work 100 percent. Even without the receipts our contractor had held onto, he insisted on honouring the 20-year warranty (and he has).

Niel is the type of small business owner who treats his work as though it is a multi-million-dollar venture. He keeps his word and is respectful of his clients. He shows up on time and does what needs to be done. We like him so much we have referred him to friends. And a year later when we needed the finishing touches, like sealing baseboards and installing cupboard doors, we asked Niel for a reference.

Enter Marie: punctual and tattooed. She's wearing jeans, a Harley Davidson jacket, and steel-toed boots. After a walkabout, she said it would take her less than a day to complete the work and she felt bad about charging us full price for such a small job. She would only charge three-quarters of her hourly rate. As we stood by the island in the kitchen chatting, she told us about the dream she'd had since she was a youngster— to employ qualified women in the construction industry. If possible, this would include single moms (or dads) who were trying to make a living while being proactive with their responsibilities as parents. Her dream included daycare as well as allowing contractors to take their kids to work occasionally. She was passionate when I asked her about her plans. The dream had grown and taken shape over many years. When she told me she had been laid off from her job, she excitedly explained it like a gift that would enable her to realize her goals.

Once we established that she could do the work required and set a price, I asked her how far along she was in getting her business established. She told us she was not looking for financing yet for the business as she had invested all of her severance pay into it. Her banker had requested a *business plan* though and she had to get that done for the next day, so she left early.

The next day, Marie was an hour and a half late. We found out that there is such a thing as Marie time and she lived in her own time zone. To her credit, her reasons for being late were always legit. On one occasion, she agreed to help her friend move furniture before she was to show up at our house, but her friend's vehicle got stuck in the mud and Marie's cell phone was in her own vehicle. She called as soon as she retrieved her phone to let us know she would arrive after she changed out of her muddy clothes. She made us laugh.

More than a month after we hired her, our minor finishing touches had still not been completed. As with most small business people, she did not have the luxury to hire people and had to do everything by herself. She had so much on her mind and so many things to do that it was difficult to keep track of everything. And she was a single mom with two kids under ten who had to deal with all the unexpected events of parenthood on her own. She was always transparent and kept us informed as to why things didn't turn out as planned and what she saw as the solution. She was prepared to live with her quote for one day of work even though she showed up at least ten times. We paid her for two days at the end of the first week as we knew from talking to her she was short of cash and needed the money to pay her rent. Marie had great intentions and we felt she would go out of her way to make sure our work was done and done well. We just did not know when.

Her business partner, Susan, who shared an apartment with Marie and her children, was also a single mom. We met Susan when she stepped in with her ex-boyfriend Mike to do some work for us when

Marie was sick. Susan replaced the screen on the front sliding door and Mike did some sanding of the baseboards that needed to be done before they were painted. Susan was also going to replace the screen on the back sliding door but needed to leave early (within about half an hour) as her daughter needed her. She suggested that I needed to clean up the balcony as her work there had created quite a mess and Mike suggested I use Marie's shop vacuum to clean up the dust he left behind when he sanded. I did clean up the balance but all I managed to do, through Mike's advice, was spread dust throughout my condominium as the shop vacuum had no filter. None of this left us with a good feeling, and we told Marie it didn't reflect well on the overall professionalism of her company.

Marie and Keith are not unlike a lot of small business people. The difference between them is that Marie has a dream and is committed to making it happen whereas Keith had neither; nor seemingly, commitment.

If you are thinking of going into business for yourself, you will likely need bank financing at some point. You will need to be able to explain your business as you will be expected to be the expert and know more about it than any lender would. In more than forty years of experience, both as a lender and an *entrepreneur*, I have found that insufficient preparation and a lack of vision are common mistakes that new business owners make. The owner of a small technology firm I once had as a customer of the bank didn't think it through when he decided to have his product manufactured in India. The invention was a winner but one day the manufacturer didn't return phone calls or ship his product. His once-promising company couldn't even meet payroll and went out of business.

As this example demonstrates, you might have the vision and a viable product but if you are ill-prepared your business is fated for failure. Before you set up your own shop and borrow from your bank, there are some basic rules to consider.

Rule number one:

If you're going into business with partners, make sure you understand them on more than a personal level.

People act differently when money's involved. Discuss the venture to ensure you can trust them to live up to their commitments and do what is best for the business. Agree on and commit to what each of you is prepared and able to do before proceeding. A written contract is always preferable but some rely on a verbal agreement. Whichever you decide on, make sure that all partners understand roles and responsibilities and are capable and willing to perform.

Rule number two:

Make sure you understand up-front the rights and responsibilities that go with each form of business

A *corporation* or a *partnership*, for example. Get some expert advice to make sure you understand what you and the other owners can and cannot do and who can make decisions about the business. It is always harder to undo the damage if things do not work out because you did not understand what you were getting into.

$$$$$$$

My partner and I believe in small business. Jack has been self-employed since 1988 and I joined his company in 1999. We are a management consulting company that specializes in advising small businesses and training lenders on how to lend to business. We are lucky enough to have the experience to advise other small businesses and are interested in helping them be successful.

Marie had been referred by Niel and through their conversations he let her know that we would be prepared to help her. The second time she came to do some work she brought her *business plan* and we reviewed it with her. She'd downloaded a template from a website and filled in the blanks but knowing what is important to include is critical. Marie and Susan had failed to include their past experience. Your banker is like a client with one critical difference: you are asking them to lend you money to help in your business and they want to get it back. Most clients don't usually see the *business plan* but a lender needs to know precisely why a prospective client should hire you and your company. Client experience is what motivates people to pay you and ultimately is the basis of how the bank gets repaid. Marie's *business plan* was built from the heart but didn't include what any lender or investor needs to know.

Lenders, like clients, rely a lot on the *character* of their borrowers. They need to know who you and your partners are. Why should they "hire" you? Are you the only one qualified to do the job? What have you done that makes you especially suited for the work and shows that you can do what you say you can? Provide examples of your accomplishments. If you can, provide references from previous jobs that speak to your qualifications. Tell the lender what you have done that sets you apart from the competition. You need to brag about yourself and your skills. That's difficult for most people, but it's essential.

When we needed to repair some ageing electronic equipment, Kent came to the house to assess our needs. As we chatted, we learned that he and a friend wanted to start their own business repairing and restoring old, and sometimes antique, electronic equipment. They had a passion for what they wanted to do but faced a great deal of competition from other small businesses as well as major electronic shops. We offered to review their *business plan*. They had been doing this for over twenty-five years and were the only people in the province certified to do these kinds of repairs, but they neglected to include this information in their *business plan*. Your ability to sell your product or yourself is what ultimately generates revenues and pays back loans. You need to highlight the important experience of each owner in the *business plan* and then attach everyone's resumes to provide detailed information.

Credit history is a big determinant in establishing a relationship with your banker. Your personal credit history is a good predictor of how you will deal with money your company borrows. If you are just starting in business, it is the only credit history available and your creditworthiness will be based on that. If your business is not a start-up, the history of living up to the commitments of previous businesses will be looked at as well.

If you do not have a good credit history it will be far more difficult to convince your banker that you are a good candidate to repay loans. If a lender does lend you money, he or she will likely need the back up of a friend or family member with a good credit history to *guarantee* the loans. That simply means that not only you and your business are responsible to repay the loans, but so is the individual that gives the *guarantee*. That's where Susan came in as she had an unblemished credit history.

Marie and Susan had been in construction for many years, primarily in new home construction. While they had worked for different companies in the distant past, they worked together in their last job. They focussed on making sure a new buyer moved into the place he or she expected. Each had different skills and Marie told us that when they decided to join forces they agreed she would be the worker and Susan would develop the *business plan* and head up the marketing side of the business.

But after several months, Marie was working hard to gain a foothold into the industry, while Susan was becoming disillusioned because the business wasn't making money and she was not holding up her part of the bargain. Rather than building a *business plan* herself, she wanted to pay someone to develop one. Marie tried to hold Susan accountable for her part of the business "*partnership*" and told her that Jack and I were prepared to help her. Susan did not respond well and thought it better to pay someone to build it. Marie admitted that previous employers and many friends were skeptical about Susan's abilities and work ethic and she was now starting to see why. Marie was now talking about buying Susan out but was concerned about damaging their friendship. Make sure you live by Rule Number One!

What happened here is common. Friends or associates decide to go into business without understanding and defining the basic business and legal concepts of what they are embarking on. They believe the inevitable rough spots will be smoothed over and solved by the friendship. The business is more likely to put a terrible strain on the friendship or even destroy it.

It is important to understand the rights and obligations that come with different forms of business. Marie's original *business plan* referred to her and Susan as "partners with a fifty percent interest each." It was not explicit about the legal form of organization they had opted for. There are several forms of legal organization but three are the most common for small businesses. I'll talk briefly about them here and describe a *limited partner, joint venture, limited liability partnership* and *limited liability corporation* in more detail at the end of the chapter.

Sole proprietorship: You are going into business as an individual and your personal assets are not separate from the business. Everything you own is in your name, not in the name of the business.

- You will pay taxes on any *profits* from the business and will be personally responsible for any losses or other obligations such as paying for supplies or repaying a bank loan.
- Anyone doing business with the proprietorship has the right to sue you and the courts can force you to sell personal assets that are outside of the business to ensure settlement of any lawsuit.
- The proprietorship ends when you end it or die.

Partnership: Two or more individuals (known as partners) pool their talents and go into business together.

- Similar to a *sole proprietorship* except that it has two or more partners that are fully responsible for any obligations of the *partnership*.
- The partners are taxed personally on their share of the *profits* (or get a tax benefit for losses).
- Any partner can commit the *partnership* to obligations without the knowledge of the other partners but every partner is on the hook for all commitments. Anyone dealing with any of the partners does not know what that *partnership* agreement says and has the legal right to take at face value what any of the

partners say. In a proprietorship, you alone are the face of the business. In a *partnership*, all partners are and each partner is as responsible for all commitments any partner makes.

- A *partnership* ceases to exist when any one of the partners exits the relationship. If any partner moves on or dies and the business continues to operate, it creates a new *partnership* if there are at least two individuals. If not, it will become a *sole proprietorship*.

Corporation: Although it costs more to establish a *corporation* than a *sole proprietorship* or *partnership*, doing business under an incorporated company does have some advantages. As a general principle:

- A *corporation* is a legal entity and the shareholders simply own shares. Whether they are involved in management or not, the shareholders invest in the company and are not otherwise responsible for what the company does. A shareholder's personal assets are not available to settle company commitments unless a side agreement is signed by the shareholder. As an example, a bank will generally require a personal *guarantee* to support loans to a *corporation* and in that case, personal assets can be used to settle corporate commitments.

- Owners who are also employees of the company will be treated like any other employee. Salaries to owners are taxed differently than dividends so you need to get professional advice on which is the most appropriate for you as an owner.
- A *corporation* continues in existence until it is shut down by the shareholders who own the shares at the time. The ownership of the shares can change hands and the *corporation* will continue on.
- In Canada, there is only one form of *corporation*, but in the U.S. there are three.

What form you decide on will depend on your circumstances and your motivations for going into business. You need to ask yourself questions, including about the industry you are in (for example, is it environmentally risky?) and the type of work you do (for example, is it subject to lawsuits?). Is the business one that will continue to exist after you retire? Do you want to pass it on to your kids? If you are unsure which is best for you, get legal advice. That will cost you, but it could save you from unexpected, expensive consequences in the long term.

Marie had set up her business as a *corporation*; she and Susan each owned half of the company. In legal terms, they were both shareholders with half the shares and an equal say in decisions affecting the company. That may seem fair, but it has some pitfalls. The business was Marie's idea and one that had been her dream for many years. So much of the value in small business is the owner and her passion. She shared the ownership of her idea with her good friend Susan by making her a fifty percent shareholder, at no cost, without understanding the implications.

Marie is a trusting person who needs to deal with her business on a practical, rather than personal, basis. Perhaps she should have considered ownership as a reward at some point in the future for Susan's commitment and performance. You need to fully understand your business partner as just that. A business partner and a friend often have conflicting viewpoints. Marie put her business idea at risk as there was nothing in the establishment of her company that put her in the driver's seat. If each shareholder owns fifty percent of the company, both shareholders have to agree to any changes or nothing will happen as neither has a controlling interest. If Marie owned more than half of the shares or through some other provision of the shareholder agreement, she could make decisions even if Susan did not agree. Given Susan's lack of commitment, as it turned out, this would have been a good idea. Jack and I are equal partners in the business but it is documented that he has the final vote when it comes to a disagreement between us.

I consulted for a trucking company that had a husband and wife as equal shareholders. When the marriage split up she retained her ownership and he was torn because he did all of the work but she got half of the *profits*. It almost ended up bankrupting the company.

Unfortunately, Marie and Susan had equal voting rights in the company, so neither could do anything without the agreement of the other. They were married in the business sense.

Let's put that into practical terms. Susan wanted to move to Ontario and open a branch of the company there. She felt it would be a successful venture because of the contacts she had there. But, Marie explained she did not want to expand the business, particularly when Susan, who had not shown a lot of motivation, would be in charge of the new venture. I told Marie that as a fifty percent shareholder she had veto rights. Susan could not expand the company without Marie's consent.

The decision to expand or not is always an important one but even more so in a fledgling company without a lot of financial flexibility. Marie needed to understand that expansion could affect the future viability of her company. First, it was their company that would be expanding into Ontario, not Susan's alone. An expansion can affect the reputation and finances of the whole company. Any commitments Susan made were commitments of the *corporation*. She would not be personally liable, but the company would. And, if the company lost money as a result of the expansion it would drain any resources from the company as a whole. A disastrous expansion into Ontario could bring the company down even if the business were successful in Alberta.

You have to fully know and be in sync with your business partner or partners, to understand the particular role and experience and commitment of each individual. You also have to understand your rights and responsibilities based on whether the company is a *partnership* or *corporation*. Most importantly for customers, you need to know what is important to them and do what you said you would do. Be respectful of their time and investment. Living in your own time zone, as Marie did when she didn't show up at the specified time, does not qualify. Few customers would be as understanding as we were. Getting all of these things right adds credibility to your business and, ultimately, is important in the decision to lend your company money.

Marie had a big decision to make.

$$$$$$$

Marie asked my advice about buying out Susan. Her new partner in life was prepared to buy into her company to provide the cash. Marie was prepared to pay a significant amount to Susan to ensure their friendship was maintained. This was a bad approach for at least two reasons. Involving her new partner was simply exacerbating what had already happened except now there was a romantic involvement, not only friendship at stake. In addition, Susan had put little cash into the company and the only value was in the idea and any contracts or individuals acting as references were the results of Marie's efforts. A financial statement of the company would likely show that the company had no value although it could have had significant future potential. But, that potential likely had nothing to do with Susan. Marie had a checkered credit history. Susan's good credit history was likely all she brought to the company and she had since added little value. There would likely need to be a negotiation to determine the amount, if any, she should be paid for her shares.

The company was about to sign a potentially lucrative contract. Marie and I discussed the structure of the contract and how she could protect herself. Within a day, I got a text message from Marie that she and Susan were to meet that day to sign the contract. Should she approach Susan about buying her out before or after the contract was negotiated and signed? She had been awake the entire night worrying about hurting her friend. My advice was to have the meeting and sign the contract without raising the issue of a potential change in ownership with Susan. Marie needed to be sure of her approach with Susan before she broached the subject.

Signing a contract for a company does not imply ownership or personal responsibility. There is a big difference between being a shareholder of a company and being a signing authority, that is, able to sign contracts on its behalf. A signing authority is a document that is used by the bank, and others, to determine who can commit the company. In this case, both Marie and Susan were signing authorities for the company and both had to sign for any document to be legally binding. Because the contract was with the company, Marie and Susan were simply signing on its behalf. If at some point they were no longer shareholders and someone else owned the company, the contract would still be valid.

The difference between shareholders and signing authorities is often misunderstood. Shareholders own the company and may or may not be involved in the business. Signing authorities, on the other hand, have the right to commit the company, but in doing so, they are not committing themselves. Think about a publicly-traded company—the company's commitment stands whether the players change or not.

Marie and Susan did sign the contract as signatories. However, not long after that Susan moved to Ontario and did not live up to her commitments either in the business or personally. She admitted that she was working for cash and pocketing the money rather than providing it to Marie for the company. She skipped out without paying rent and her share of expenses. To Marie's credit, she approached the Corporate Registry of Alberta and managed to have Susan removed as a shareholder of the company. She called the police and found out she could tape the conversation with Susan which highlighted that Susan was leaving town and giving up her interest in the company. Marie played the tape for the registry and that was sufficient to remove Susan as a shareholder. She now says she will never have another person as a shareholder in her company and will be totally responsible for any decisions. She has opted not to have her partner invest in the business and is relying instead on help from others in the form of advice and work, not cash. It is likely where she should have been in the first place had she fully understood the implications before she entered into the arrangement with Susan. On the negative side, Marie had not had time to cultivate any business and was behind on her bills when Susan left. Even the potentially lucrative contract was cancelled by the other party, no doubt when they got wind of the shareholder dispute.

Marie is still trying to get a foothold into the industry. She has managed to get some contracts and with the help of her advisers should be able to continue to pursue her dream. We did keep working with her to help guide her in the right direction but have since lost touch with her. The last we heard, she was hired by a contractor to help build the business, but that relationship didn't work out so I suspect she is back at trying to build her own business.

Marie's experience is similar to many small businesses and points out **why it is so important to make the right decisions early on**. She was lucky to regain control of her company but it was at a significant cost. She had to focus on that rather than operating her business and building revenues, and that could have been the end of her business.

The decisions you make early have everlasting effects on your company and they are not all necessarily positive. You need to fully understand yourself and your motivations and communicate those to any partners you have and your banker. Make sure you choose the people that will work with you carefully and ensure you all understand respective roles and duties. The legal form of your business (*sole proprietorship, partnership, corporation,* etc.) will drive a lot of the decisions you make, so get advice before you choose. If Marie had known to seek such advice, she might have avoided a great deal of heartache and cost, and been further ahead today in realizing her dream.

ADDENDUM

Other types of organizations that are not as common in small business include:

Limited partnerships: *Limited partners* are treated differently than *general partners*, or those that operate the business. Some *partnerships* have both *general partners* and *limited partners*.

- A *general partner* can commit the *partnership* and has unlimited liability for the obligations of the *partnership*.
- A *limited partner* invests money in the business but is not otherwise involved. In that instance, and only if it can be proven that the *limited partner* is not actively involved in the management of the *partnership*, the *limited partners* will not likely be responsible for more than the amount invested. A *limited partner* is treated similarly to a shareholder in a *corporation*.

Joint ventures: *Joint ventures* are legal organizations formed for the purpose of completing a project.

- Each partner contributes either assets or management expertise (or a combination of both) to the *joint venture* in return for a share of the *profits*.
- Partners pay taxes on their portion of any

profits (or can use losses as a deduction for tax purposes).
- A *joint venture* ceases to exist when the project is completed and the assets and cash are distributed.

Limited liability partnerships *(LLPs):* LLPs are similar to a *partnership* except that the individual partners are responsible only for things that they are directly involved with.
- Law firms and accounting firms often organize as LLPs to ensure that if one lawyer or accountant is sued, the legal liability is limited to that individual, not the entire firm.
- LLPs are quite common in all states of the U.S. but only some Canadian jurisdictions allow them.

Limited liability corporations *(LLCs):* LLCs are not allowed in Canada but are common in the U.S.
- LLCs are a hybrid between *partnerships* and *corporations*. LLCs are not incorporated but do limit the liability of the members, or shareholders.
- Any income or losses are declared personally by the partners.

Chapter 2

Where Do You Go to Get Money and How Do You Get There?

Kent and his friend John were techno wizards and had a passion for sound equipment. They played with the stuff when they were kids and continued to do so in the evenings even after they became fully employed by others—still in the tech business but not involved in sound equipment. They wanted to turn that passion into their own business. They planned to repair old equipment, sell amplifiers, and take advantage of the renewed interest in vinyl. Kent had designed and manufactured his own amps that were better quality and much cheaper than the competition. It might have taken some convincing for those who weren't sound aficionados to repair old equipment as it often costs less to buy new, but they were relying on nostalgia.

Kent worked for a security company. He had hurt his back when he slipped and fell off a ladder and knew he would be laid off as he couldn't meet all the physical requirements of his job. John was working but felt that the quality of work the company produced was not what he was capable of. Kent worked at the sound business in his spare time but wanted to turn his hobby into a full-time job. Both needed an income as Kent had a young family and John supported himself. Neither of them had a lot of cash to invest so they needed someone else to provide much-needed money.

They had a great idea and the requisite skills to make a successful business but needed to take the next step and find financing. Most people go to a bank first but that may not be the best place to start.

Where you decide to go depends on how much you need, what you have to offer, and what's in it for the person providing the money. Kent and John needed to think about what they needed. To convince someone to give or lend them money, they needed to understand the business and be prepared to answer any questions they might be asked.

$$$$$$$

Kent and John knew why they wanted to go into business and what they had to offer and the *business plan* they developed needed to tell their perspective financier that. Knowing what to include in your plan goes back to why you are in business. Most people don't decide to set out on their own because they like accounting. In over forty years, I have never met one who did (unless their specialty was accounting) and the comment bankers often hear is I do *financial statements* only because you need them. It is not your reason to be in business but if you don't care how well you're doing, it will be harder to convince others to give you money. You need to look at it as a scorecard. Are you winning or losing? Do you understand why and can you explain it?

There are many reasons why folks decide to become self-employed. Most need to pay the bills but other motivations are varied. I have seen so many different scenarios—some, like Niel, do not want to and cannot work for others; some, like Marie, have a dream they want to fulfill or the satisfaction of building a company; some, like Kent, see a niche that is not satisfied; and some just need a job. Most are good at what they do—they produce the best widgets. Others have a great new idea. I look at this distinction as what separates small business owners and *entrepreneurs*.

Many *entrepreneurs* are small business owners, but most small business owners are not *entrepreneurs*. Many chief executive officers of large companies are *entrepreneurs* so it is not size that differentiates them, it is how they think.

When I talk about an *entrepreneur*, I am describing "someone who tries something and if it doesn't work just picks himself up, dusts himself off and tries something else." There is quite a difference between the two styles and they present very different challenges to the self-employed as well as their bankers.

Small business owners don't typically have the confidence that *entrepreneurs* do. They look at what they do as an extension of themselves and if the business falters, they believe they are failures. In my first lending job, I financed the renovations for a restaurant. It was a fine dining restaurant that had a tired décor so the renovations were designed to update the interior to match the menu. The owners didn't know how to negotiate or manage a construction budget and neither did I at the time. The renovations were fraught with cost overruns as everything took longer and cost more than anticipated. The restaurant went into bankruptcy because it could not pay for the cost overruns. Both owners felt like failures even though they had what many believed to be the best food and service in town. They took it personally and so did I. I learned a lot from that experience but the relationship and trust with them became paramount. I was a *character* reference for them when they approached another bank in the future to finance a new restaurant. What happened had nothing to do with their skills as restauranteurs—something they should have stuck to. Hiring someone to negotiate and manage the renovations would have possibly saved their restaurant.

Understanding whether you are an *entrepreneur* or

a small business person will define the risks you are prepared to take. Small business owners typically stick to what they know. *Entrepreneurs* thrive on trying new things. Medhi was a great cook and owned a restaurant that started as a fine dining halal Persian restaurant that was not licensed. When the economy slowed down, he added alcohol to the menu to generate more sales and food that is not halal—things like pepperoni pizza. He added televisions with the paid sports channel in a section of the restaurant. He was an *entrepreneur* and prepared to change his operation and try new things to keep his restaurant in business in a slow economy. He has since passed the restaurant on to his son who has added an outside deck. Medhi was ever the *entrepreneur* and has since opened a pizza and chicken take-out place.

Entrepreneurs can be difficult to manage but also successful. They often ignore the rules. Many live on the premise it is better to ask for forgiveness than approval. When I was a banker, only twice did I run across such *entrepreneurs* and I suggested we ask both to find a new bank. Both were profitable and doing well. Only problem was they didn't do what they said they would and it was only a matter of time before things went wrong. It is one thing if you don't understand because your banker doesn't do a good job in telling you what you need to know. It is different to understand and ignore, which is what both of these *entrepreneurs* did. Both signed an agreement that they would not spend over a certain amount of money without talking to the bank first. Both did—one purchased a building and one a business. Your reputation is what lenders rely on and if what you do blemishes that, you may not be able to get money in the future. I have since heard that one company is still with the bank and having financial problems. The other company was bought out so at least they didn't hit the wall as I predicted.

Kent and John were small business people and wanted to earn a living by doing something they loved and were good at. It never got to the point where they approached a bank for money, but I suspect they were the type to follow the rules that they signed into, unless of course they didn't understand them. If you don't get it, ask.

$$$$$$$

We told Kent we would help him with his *business plan* and he and John came to the house one day to discuss what they had put on paper. We gave them some ideas on how to make it resonate with the readers.

First, build your plan around you and brag about your skills and accomplishments. Sell yourself first and foremost. The credibility of your *business plan* depends on that. Summarize what you have done and attach a resume to give more detail.

Make your plan realistic and be clear about what you did to develop it. Believe and satisfy yourself that you can achieve what you say you can. Nobody wins if you don't and you will be the biggest loser. Think about why people would choose your product or service over the competition. I lent to an Italian ice cream parlour that was the only one in town that served authentic Italian ice cream. It was made from cream (I found out not all ice cream is) and used a secret recipe handed down through generations. Its success was based on the quality and uniqueness of the product and they marketed their business on that. They were so successful they wanted to open a second store before the first one was a year old. There wasn't enough history so I told them to wait until the existing store was proven. They didn't want to and managed to get another bank to lend them the money but only if they mortgaged their house. The business failed and they not only lost their business but also their house. Listen to advice before you make up your mind. It could save you.

A *business plan* is your road map and you need to tell how you developed it. You might not create your own *business plan*. There are organizations that will do that for you complete with a glossy cover and graphics but you have to understand everything that is in it. Your credibility is at stake if you are asked questions about your *business plan* and the only answer is that someone else put it together. Never forget, it is your business and your plan. A *business plan* without assumptions is simply a sheet of paper full of numbers. It is like a bicycle without wheels—it will get you nowhere. For example, if your plan includes sales, how do you calculate them? How many units can you sell and at what price? How does that compare with your competition? Is your product more expensive, cheaper, or the same price as theirs and what differentiates it? Why would users purchase your product and not theirs? You need to tell the readers where your numbers came from and how and why they make sense.

The first draft of Kent's *business plan* had some great information in it but was also missing important details. He and John had worked on it for some time. Their passion was sound equipment but they knew in order to attract investors they needed to sell their idea. The "devil was in the details" best describes his first effort. It looked great but he had not described how he got there. I once had a senior staff member tell me he didn't bother to look at *business plan*s as he didn't believe them. He had never seen one that didn't work. They all showed the company could be successful. Convince anyone reading the plan why it will be successful. As one colleague put it, "Let them agree with you."

Kent's Executive Summary described his products and services and how many satisfied and returning clients he'd had in the thirty days since the business started. He outlined the benefits of working with his company and provided a summary of his financial *projections*.

Kent provided sales figures without justification as to how they were developed. He had to include in his plan what he told us—he had revenue from sales, repairs, and manufacturing and his starting point was revenue generated when the business was a hobby. Because he worked full time, he had only about ten hours a week to spend on it. He researched the market and came up with what he believed the total demand for his product was and who his competition was. He based his sales *projections* on that as well as the business he needed to turn away when he worked part-time. He didn't have time to complete all the projects that came his way but if he were to turn his hobby into a full-time business, the rejected projects would become revenue. Suddenly, his numbers had some credibility and no longer seemed like they were pulled out of thin air. He said in his *business plan* that he decreased his original sales numbers by 15 percent to be conservative. That showed that he had put some thought into it.

Kent also explained the direct costs associated

with his sales. He shopped the competition to understand what he could sell products for and had contacted potential suppliers to find out how much he had to pay for them. *Profit* was based solely on the difference between the two and was a small part of his business. For repairs, the parts were minimal but labour was extensive. When he got busier and had to hire employees, he likely would have to pay them an hourly wage so he would need to better understand how long each job would take and build that into his costs. At the start, because he and his partner were the only employees and on a salary, the amount they were paid would not change regardless of how long it took to complete a repair. What would change though was how much new business they could take on if they hadn't estimated the time correctly. Unfortunately, there is no such thing as a "typical" repair and so much depends on the job itself. Kent's opinion was it would take an employee longer than he or his partner as they were certified and had been doing it for a long time.

On the manufacturing side, he had designed an amplifier and had been producing it for years. It had a better sound and cost about half of what his competitor offered. He sourced parts from the most cost-competitive vendor. He knew other places he could get them if that vendor was unable to supply him. He had a back-up plan. The guy he usually bought from could have his own supply problems or even shut down. If that happened and Kent couldn't get the parts he needed, he would have to put his manufacturing on hold until he found a new supplier. He could explain how much money he would make on each unit sold.

Had Kent included the sales and cost information it would have built a lot of credibility. Anyone looking at the original plan might assume that he hadn't thought much about it and had no justification for his projected sales or *cost of goods sold*. I advised him to include the details in the next draft of his *business plan*.

If your business works on contracts, use them as the starting point for the sales you think you can achieve and explain what you are doing. Existing contracts ensure revenues, provided you do what you are supposed to do, and show that you have garnered the trust of clients. They make your *business plan* believable. Include other contracts you have bid on. If you won a contract, explain what your competitive advantages were and why you won. If you lost, understand why. You want to make sure you know how to bid similar contracts in the future so you don't lose out to a competitor. That tells people you know your competition and how to use your strengths to win future contracts. Include any outstanding bids as they could be a source of revenue. My advice always is to include two scenarios—what you know and what is potential and why your outstanding bids should be successful. What actually happens will fall somewhere between the two.

Finding money for a start-up business is more difficult than for established ones. If you have no history of sales or contracts, it is harder to persuade others how and why you will be successful. Know your competition and what they offer. Why will you win sales over them? You need a compelling argument to convince investors or lenders your business can succeed.

What it costs to run your business depends on whether you operate out of your house or not. If you are home-based, your plan will look different than if you are looking to fund the stand-alone costs of the operation on top of what you need to pay to keep your home running. If you are operating from another location, you need to build in costs like rent, utilities, and insurance on the premises. If the business is the only source of income for you and your family, you need to pay yourself enough to cover personal expenses. While there is no rule of thumb when it comes to how much to pay yourself, you need to understand that draining your business to support your lifestyle is counterproductive. If there are other sources of income like a working spouse or rental income that limit the amount you need to be paid, explain that and include how much and from where. If things don't turn out as planned, do you have other sources of cash as a back-up?

Include all costs. If the business is regional or international, consider the costs of delivery options and timing. If you sell your product or purchase internationally, consider foreign exchange implications. What currency will you sell in? How will the value of the Canadian dollar affect demand for the product as well as cash flow? What strategy do you have in place to make sure you are still making money if the value of the dollar changes? The trucking industry came up with a great solution when the price of gas increased. They added a rider to their contracts. If gas went up, customers paid more and if it went down, they paid less. The companies made sure they made a *profit* on their delivery capabilities. If a trucker loses money on each trip because the price of gas went up, even if the customer is happy he can't stay in business long. That became the standard in the industry so it was not a competitive disadvantage. If you are going to implement something similar, understand your competition first. If your contracts have a price adjustment built-in and none of your competitors do, you could lose business. If you are losing money because of something beyond your control like a change in the value of a currency, it might be better to lose the business.

Kent and his partner did a great job of detailing and explaining the monthly costs to run the business. They did not plan to work out of the house so they needed to provide a list of expenses. Provide as much detail as you can so anyone reviewing the plan knows if there is anything not included and ask questions. Kent and John didn't include their salaries so the cash was left in the business, and the *profits* were overstated. There was also no mention made of the costs of doing business throughout North America, although that was part of the plan. I told them they needed to add in salaries and think about currency implications and build that in so that there would be no surprises.

The revenue and expense numbers tell you and other investors and lenders what you expect to generate as *profit* and what is leftover at the end of the year.

Figure out and explain how much you will need to come up with to start the business and how much cash you can put into the company. Most people underestimate how much start-up expenses like incorporation costs (how much you pay to get your company set up), advertising, including business cards and tools and equipment. Kent's didn't include incorporation costs but provided a detailed listing of what was needed to start the business, including his existing tools and equipment. The money already spent would be considered as part of your cash in the company. In some cases, "sweat equity" can also be considered. Kent didn't include the time he spent developing the amp or sourcing parts for it and he should have. Having "skin in the game" is positive—any lender or investor will expect you to have put your own money in. It shows your commitment and assures them that if the business fails, they will not be the only ones to lose. Walking away is easier when you have nothing to lose. When Marie started her own renovation business, she invested vacation pay from her previous job and the money she spent on her tools of the trade. As a single mom with no other source of income, that showed a lot of commitment.

A well thought out plan says how much you think you can generate in cash. In a start-up, you don't really know. Even if you have an existing operation and things are changing, because you are adding new products or expanding to a new location, the future is uncertain. Your *business plan* needs to explain everything you have considered when you decided to go into a new venture or expand your existing one. For example, if you project your revenues will increase, explain how and why. How much will it cost and what are you doing differently to generate the increase? Business follows a common rule—if you expect the results to change, you have to change the way you do things.

Numbers are important and family members, investors, lenders, or grant providers need to know they make sense. I once asked a banker what he thought of the *projections* provided by his client. He hadn't looked at them. They were done without the thoughts of "what if?" and did not show they had thought through the ramifications. The banker didn't believe most plans made sense. Make sure yours does.

Businesses often underestimate how much money they need. That can be the result of poor planning but sometimes it just takes longer to get set up and generate revenues. Even the best plan is not immune to unexpected costs. Your *business plan* will become a scorecard and a measure of your success. How close are your actual results to what you thought you could do? If significantly different, do you understand why and can you explain it? If you can, that shows you understand your business and builds confidence in your abilities.

$$$$$$$

Once we spoke, Kent had an idea of what he needed to add to his *business plan* based on the research he had done. However, numbers are not the only thing you need in a *business plan*. Explain how you will market your business and who your potential customers are. Is your market local, regional, or international and how are you going to reach those potential clients? Build a detailed marketing plan. Will you use social media, do you have a website, do you have references from past customers, can you use special events to promote your product, can and will existing customers refer people to you? A business owner needs to understand the best way to reach customers. Social media and websites are becoming more prominent because of the wide audience they reach. If you market that way, narrow down which sites you will use so you don't spread yourself too thin. Make sure the site always works and keep it up to date. Be interactive.

Kent's marketing plan was well thought out. He would use social media and word of mouth. He would use a website that his friend in Ontario, a website guru, would enhance and use it to sell the company in that market as well. On the social media side, he had joined some audio and music groups and told us how he connected with potential audiences that increased the number of hits to his own website. In return for supporting special interest groups through ticket sales and fliers, potential clients would be directed to his website. He wanted to export to the U.S. and the social media and the internet would cross borders so if he wanted to exploit that market, the advertising was already there. He was clear about what sites he would engage in but didn't detail which ones or explain what he would do to keep them up to date. He needed to paint a picture. He needed to include his friend in Ontario that was a website guru in his plan and what implications that would have for website design and keeping things up to date.

$$$$$$$

Once Kent made the suggested changes, his *business plan* would be polished and ready to go. Before he used it as a tool to raise money, he needed to give it to trusted friends, family, and advisers to review to make sure he hadn't missed anything. That's what both Kent and Marie did with us on a first pass and we made suggestions. Once the *business plan* has passed muster with the other folks, you need to figure out the best way to finance your start-up or help you continue in your business.

There are various sources and ways to structure that investment.

- Friends and family are the primary source of money for a lot of small start-up businesses. Those folks just want to help you out by lending you money or investing in your company. Unless they gift you the money, they hope to get it back.
- Equity investors will provide cash in return for ownership in your company. As a small business person, you are an equity investor in your company and often the only investor. If not, family and friends may provide cash in return for shares or you may persuade others to invest. Some equity investors get involved

in the management of the company and some only in the overall direction the company will take.
- Lenders provide loans and are paid interest on those loans. They cannot get involved in the management of the company.

These three in addition to *grants* are basically the different sources for money and everybody has a different reason for writing a cheque. Understand the reason and consider it before you make the pitch. There are two extremes—the moral desire to help people and to make money. The reasons span the whole range and in some cases, both motivations come to play.

Grants are typically from governments or organizations that want to encourage jobs or have an interest in providing support if you have a great idea in a particular type of business. As long as your company lives up to the terms and *conditions* of the grant, it typically does not have to be repaid.

Lenders cover the whole spectrum as well. The motivation for *micro-loans* is far-reaching but lean more to helping an individual or business succeed. A married couple we know provides financing for *micro-loans* internationally. The organization has made loans in over fifty countries. While they both provide money, their investment objectives are different. Rose is a retired health care professional who has a clear desire to help others but she will only reinvest once she is repaid. She wants to limit her downside to her initial investment. Todd retired from the oil patch about ten years ago and spends his time volunteering in the community. His activities range from greeting visitors at the airport to conducting Board Governance seminars for volunteer boards. He continues to add to his investments when he sees potential. The smallest loan Rose made was $65 to enable a young lady in the Middle-East to buy a goat. The motivation is definitely not to make money. They have a moral desire to help people. They do not want to lose the amount they initially invested but are prepared to take that risk if it will help others. Banks are considered to be at the other extreme of lenders. Their primary goal is to be paid back as they are simply renting out the money of depositors and shareholders. On a secondary basis, they do want to make a modest return and also help businesses succeed.

Angel investors and *Venture capital* are prepared to invest in risky ventures but expect to be well paid for the risk they take. Angels get involved in the management of the company and *Venture capital* typically provide guidance but do not get involved in day to day management. The television show The Dragon's Den is a great example of *Venture capital*. A member of the panel may write a cheque in return for ownership in the company if they see potential to make money. That's not to say the investors are not interested in helping a business succeed, just that it is not their primary goal for writing the cheque.

$$$$$$$

The moral of the story is you need to know your business better than anyone else and the only way you can do that is to research the potential market, understand your competition and what your costs will be. Kent knew his business well and did his research but he did not do a great job of explaining that in his original *business plan*. Jack and I met with him when we needed more of our old sound systems updated and he had found a job in the security business that used his electronics skills but also provided the certainty of an income he needed for his family. I can't help but think that developing his *business plan* and understanding his marketable skills was the reason he was able to promote himself and find a job in an economy that was floundering.

Chapter 3

Why Cash is King!

Which numbers are important, why and what do they mean?

When I was in the loan approval department the first time in the early 1980s, Maureen and I were not only the first women that I knew to be responsible for reviewing loans but we were among the first folks that had lending experience and had been account managers. She had been a banker for far longer than I—about eighteen years compared to my three years. The credit analyst jobs, as they were referred to then, were considered training for those who wanted to lend money. I can only imagine the frustration from those facing the customer relying on someone who never had faced a client to decide whether to recommend the loan or not. The questions were often not relevant but unfortunately, the answers decided whether the request for a loan for the client would be approved. We had some experience on that front and although we had no lending limit at the time we were responsible for writing up the responses for the two Vice Presidents that ran the department. You had to know which one would be responsible to sign off on the loan as the writing—and lending styles—of the two were very different. We reviewed whatever came in for us that day and if we finished early we helped someone else out.

My next stint in credit approval was in Special Loans in Montreal. We—and I use the word loosely—were responsible for dealing with international loans that weren't up to date on payments or were at risk of being unable to. I digress a bit to help you understand how banks have changed since those early days. Then you were tapped on the shoulder for jobs, unlike today where you have to apply for them. The Human Resources Department was responsible for career planning and they were looking for an MBA with lending experience. It seems I fit the bill and despite being warned by the Vice President who had just been transferred to the department, I left Vancouver (and my new partner) to move to Montreal for the sake of my career. I lasted all of six months, give or take, as my only job was to compile reports and read newspapers for clippings to give to the other officers. I made the mistake of insulting the officer I reported to by suggesting that the job was clerical in nature and should be rated that way. As a result, my staff report was not positive, to say the least, and was changed after I had seen it. I did call the head of Vancouver district as a friend and asked for advice. Suffice it to say, he made sure the next time I called after a visit with the personnel department (who told me they would look into moving me in a couple of years), I got approval to arrange a move back to Vancouver at the bank's expense. My personnel officer was not in when I called so the approval was given by another officer who I had not met. Obviously, the boss had intervened and I was moved back as a supernumerary—that meant the District was prepared to pay for my move and my salary even though there was not a position open for me. I'm not sure where I would be now if he hadn't intervened on my behalf. It is only fair to paint both sides of the picture—a move that went wrong and a person that made it right.

Later on in my career, after I had much more experience, I again went to the loan approval department as a deputy to the Vice President on the business side. That basically meant I was the head of business lending and there was another individual, David, who was head of personal lending in the district. I had been lending money for over fifteen years and had a ton of experience that ranged from approving small loans on my own hook to recommending them to someone else who had a higher limit. As deputy, my lending limit was $25 million when my boss was around and $50 million when he wasn't. Everything over $5 million needed two signatures so I was always working with someone on a deal either as the approver or the recommender. Our job was to decide if the bank could reasonably expect the client to repay the loan. I was busy and reviewed at least five or six applications a day and even busier when applications didn't have all the information I needed to make an informed decision. That's when I had to go back to the account managers to get it. Usually, it wasn't their fault. They typically manage between fifty and 150 clients and are juggling between ten and fifteen requests at a time. A lot of clients don't plan ahead so the applications normally had a tight time-frame and not a lot of information. If what I asked for was not in the file, the account manager had to contact the client for clarification. That process could lead to a lengthy delay in deciding on the loan. Once I had all the necessary information, I either made a decision myself or recommended to a higher level whether I thought the loan should be approved or not.

There is an old saying that Cash is King. Only cash pays back money you owe.

While roles have not changed significantly—credit approvers still approve loans and account managers recommend them—how the banks do business has. In those days, we sat in our offices dressed in pin-striped or dark business suits and clients and other bankers came to us. My first office in that job was on the Executive floor and about 120 square feet. Over time, we were moved to smaller offices on the same floor that were about one-quarter of the size and not nearly as well decorated. I buzzed the movers when I asked that my desk be put sideways so I could see the mountains. Everyone else, except the Vice President, had their back to the windows. He had a larger office so it made sense to put his desk sideways. I always had popcorn and often had a trail outside my door with account managers taking a handful on their way out. When I was transferred from that job, my boss gave a speech and acknowledged he never thought credit was humorous until he sat next door to me. Everybody who left was laughing.

We met with clients occasionally but the meetings were in the boardroom on the floor. It must have been very intimidating to them to show up on the Executive floor and be escorted into that room. I recall one such meeting when I was asked to get coffee for a customer—he thought I was a secretary and was quite amazed when the Vice President introduced me as the person responsible for analyzing and recommending whether to approve his loans or not.

Now your banker probably shares an office with others in the same position (it is called hoteling) or works at home, dresses more like clients do, and is expected to be out visiting customers. But, one thing remains the same: Anything you as a client can do to make your banker's life easier and save time helps them help you and gets the answer quicker. Providing the correct information and speaking the lingo builds the rapport and relationship.

There is quite a difference between banks and investors when it comes to the money they put into your business. Banks are in the business of lending money and expect to lose money on some loans. Remember, though, that banks have no upside if you do well. They will be paid back what they lend to you plus some interest. However, if your company does not succeed, they stand to lose what they lent you.

While investors share the same risks if you do not do well, shareholders will benefit if you do well as they will share in the *profits* of the company.

Banks want to lend to business and help them succeed but only if they believe they will be paid back with interest. You need to convince them that your business can do that. Pitch your business to your banker so they have enough information to sell it to someone else in the organization. By understanding what they look for and providing as much of that information as you can, you vastly increase your chances of success.

$$$$$$$

You need to pay attention to *financial statements* and *projections*. I will define the terms and then apply them in a practical manner.

When a small business suggests (as they often do) that they prepare *financial statements* only because they need to provide them to a lender, it raises a red flag. Every manager needs the information to make good business decisions and what they tell you is critical to your success. The numbers let you understand the basics and what your lender is looking for. Financial results are a scorecard of the success of your business but only measure what has already happened. You also need to understand where you are going and whether you have enough cash to get you there. Each investor or lender may focus on slightly different ratios but most will be concerned about *liquidity* (do you have enough cash to pay your bills) and *solvency* (do you have more assets than liabilities). We'll talk about the common terms you might hear, what they mean to you and your lender, and why they are important. It adds to your credibility (and your chances of getting a loan) if you can understand what the lender is saying.

Here is an example of a financial statement for My Manufacturing Ltd. that we'll use to show what the numbers mean and why they are important. Included on the *balance sheet* are *current assets* (assets that will provide cash within a year), *current liabilities* (money that needs to be paid within a year), *long term assets* (property, plant and equipment that are used in the business to produce sales), *long term liabilities* (money that will be paid over time) and *equity* (the amount that the shareholder(s) originally invested in the company for the purchase of shares plus any *profit* that has not been paid to the shareholders as dividends, which is called *retained earnings*).

Depreciation is on a separate line and sometimes it is simply included as a cost, and interest is shown after *operating expenses* when it is sometimes just included in overall costs. An *income statement* represents what has happened between two year-ends and in the case of My Manufacturing shows the results of the company between January 1 and December 31 in each of three years.

My Manufacturing Ltd. Balance Sheet as at December 31 ($)			
	Year 1	Year 2	Year 3
ASSETS			
Cash	16,400	2,800	17,200
Accounts receivable	110,660	89,600	116,000
Inventory	77,200	93,500	91,800
TOTAL CURRENT ASSETS	204,260	185,900	225,000
LONG TERM ASSETS			
Property, plant and equipment	168,400	249,200	319,700
Accumulated depreciation	66,500	81,600	97,500
Net Fixed Assets	101,900	167,600	222,200

TOTAL ASSETS	306,160	353,500	447,200
LIABILITIES			
CURRENT LIABILITIES			
Revolving loan—Bank	2,300	9,100	28,400
Current portion of long term debt	6,200	13,900	16,500
Accounts payable	103,200	100,500	105,900
Income taxes payable	1,700	900	0
TOTAL CURRENT LIABILITIES	113,400	124,400	150,800
LONG TERM LIABILITIES			
Long term debt	168,660	186,200	210,000
Due to shareholders	0	2,300	19,600
Deferred taxes	0	3,200	11,700
TOTAL LIABILITIES	282,060	316,100	392,100
SHAREHOLDER'S EQUITY			
Common shares	200	200	200
Retained earnings	23,900	37,200	54,900
TOTAL SHAREHOLDER'S EQUITY	24,100	37,400	55,100
TOTAL LIABILITIES AND EQUITY	306,160	353,500	447,200

My Manufacturing Ltd.
Income Statement for the period ended December 31 ($)

	Year 1	Year 2	Year 3
Sales	636,700	821,600	951,600
Cost of goods sold	451,800	607,200	729,300
Depreciation	6,500	6,500	7,000
Gross Profit	178,400	207,900	215,300
Operating expenses	146,700	171,800	171,200
Operating income	31,700	36,100	44,100
Interest expense	22,400	19,500	19,500
Net profit before taxes	9,300	16,600	24,600
Income tax provision	2,600	3,300	7,100
Net profit after tax	6,700	13,300	17,500

Cash flow

A toy manufacturer that had been in business for many years had only a slight increase in sales each year and managed to make the toys at a consistent *cost of goods sold*. Because the owner had a steady business, his banking needs did not change year to year. He didn't need any more money. A road construction company that got new contracts because business expanded and sales grew needed more money. The business expanded and as a result, his banking needs increased. Some sources and uses of cash in the business are obvious. When you sell your product or service and get paid, you get money. When you pay your suppliers, staff, rent, and of course the government, etc., you use it. If your sales are the same year after year and you make the same *profit*, if you run the business the same way, it is likely your need for cash will not change.

What does running your business the same way mean and how might your cash needs change if your revenues and expenses don't and you are making the same *profit*? First, you need to understand what a *balance sheet* means and why it is important.

The asset side of the *balance sheet* shows everything you own, including what people owe you for something you have sold them or a service you have provided (*accounts receivable*), *inventory* (the product you sell), and machinery and equipment (*fixed assets*).

On the other side of the *balance sheet* are liabilities and *equity*. Liabilities and *equity* are what provided the money to pay for the assets. Liabilities are what you owe other people—for example, your suppliers (*accounts payable*) and your bank if you have a loan (*operating loans*, notes payable or long term debt). *Equity* is what you (and other shareholders if there are any) have invested in your business either through *profits* you have earned and not paid out as dividends (*retained earnings*) or the purchase of shares.

You might also have lent money to the company and that amount is shown as shareholder loans. If you have agreed with your lender and signed what is called a *Postponement of Claim*, it means that you will leave that money in the company. It will be considered *equity*—money you have invested in the company. If not, it will be considered a liability and an amount that needs to be paid back in the normal course of business. The assets have to equal the sum of liabilities and *equity*. In the My Manufacturing Ltd. example, in all three years, the *balance sheets* balance, which is the first thing a lender will check.

According to accounting principles, there are only four basic sources and uses of cash in a business. The sources are *profit*, a decrease in assets (such as the collection of receivables or the sale of machinery and equipment), an increase in liabilities (what you owe the bank or your suppliers), and an increase in *equity* (the owner puts more money into the business). The uses are expenses, an increase in assets, a decrease in liabilities or a decrease in *equity* (the owner takes money out of the company in dividends). It is fairly straightforward, to know whether the company is making a *profit* (a source of cash) or if it is losing money (a use). The others need some demystifying.

It took me a long time to understand that an increase in *accounts receivable* was a use of cash. I got it with *inventory* because it made sense that if you bought something you have to pay for it and that uses money. But, when you think about it, if you don't get the cash when you expect it (like if you give your customers thirty days to pay and you don't receive payment for forty-five days), you need to find a way to come up with the cash you need for that extra fifteen days. That's what it means when you don't run your business the same way. You can have exactly the same *profit* and loss statement but if you don't collect your receivables as quickly as you did last year you will need more cash. The same thing goes for *inventory*. If you don't sell it as fast as you did last year or you decide to carry more *inventory*, you will have less cash.

Think about the payables side of your business. You need to pay for your product but suppliers are a free source of cash. If you pay them on time, they finance your *inventory* and it doesn't cost you anything extra. Typically, they will ask that you pay in thirty days and if you don't there could be interest added on to what you owe. If the late charge is an extra two percent, it is an expensive form of financing.

Some suppliers will offer an incentive for you to pay early. With a two percent discount if you do so within ten days, you can decrease your cost of sales by two percent. If you purchase $100,000 in *inventory* every month and receive a two percent discount, it costs you only $98,000. If you do that every month for a year, you will have an extra $24,000. Compare that to the cost of borrowing money to receive the discount. If you deduct the cost of borrowing from the amount you save, you will still be in the money. If you borrow the full $100,000, assume the interest on it for a full year is $4,000. Because you can reduce that $100,000 by any cash you receive, the borrowing costs will most likely be less than that. Overall, you can increase your bottom line by at least $20,000. That's cash in your pocket.

It may make sense to offer your customers a discount to pay early so you have your cash quicker. You'll give up some margin but if you need cash it may be a solution to a potential problem.

If you are profitable but cannot meet your bills on time or at all, something is happening. Are your customers paying you on time and if not, what are you doing about it? You have to be as diligent with collecting what you're owed as you are with making sales. If your customers meet what they owe you on time, you don't need to find the cash to replace what they didn't pay. If a customer owes you $50,000 on

April 30 and doesn't pay you until May 30, you need to find that $50,000 somewhere else to fund your operations for that 30 days.

Do you have too much *inventory* or *inventory* that is not selling? Understand your supply chain. Do you need as much *inventory* on hand as you have or could you manage it differently? Is the *inventory* readily available so you can order it on a just-in-time basis or do you need a long lead time? A bakery should manage its *inventory* purchases—its *raw materials* like flour when they need it as it is not in shortage and can be delivered right away. A manufacturer that imports parts from China will need to order in advance and maintain sufficient *inventory* to meet production targets. If you can reduce your *inventory* (without suffering a decrease in sales), you'll free up cash. Your suppliers are a source of free money and extra cash if you pay them early. So, manage your business and not just your sales. If you have too much invested in *inventory* or are not collecting your *accounts receivable* in a timely manner, you may not be able to pay your suppliers, or worse your staff.

The same concepts apply in a growing business but there are other challenges including the need for additional cash. If sales are increasing, the rule of thumb is that receivables, *inventory*, and payables will increase by a similar percentage. The operating cycle of a business is how long it takes to go from cash to cash—the number of days it takes to purchase *inventory* (create an *accounts payable*), make a sale, pay for *inventory* (settle an *accounts payable*), and receive cash (collect an *accounts receivable*).

The *financing gap* is the difference between the sum of receivables and *inventory* less payables and that is the amount of money you need to come up with to make sure you can pay your suppliers. In other words, it's the amount you need to finance your operating cycle. Arc Productions was a Canadian animation studio based in Toronto that did the background on such films as Lost in Oz and special effects on Before I Wake. It grew itself out of business. In a year and a half, it doubled its staff to keep up with demand but did not have enough cash to pay its bills and in August 2016 ended up with a *liquidity* problem and had to sell to a competitor. As one unnamed senior staff member said, "They grew too big, too fast." If you are planning to grow sales by 10 percent a year, you will need more cash. If last year's receivables were $60,000, *inventory* was $50,000 and payables were $40,000, the *financing gap* was $70,000 (receivables plus *inventory* less payables). If you increase sales by 10 percent, each account will increase by approximately 10 percent so the *financing gap* becomes $77,000 ($66,000 plus $55,000 less $44,000). That means you need to come up with $7,000 more just to finance your operations. That doesn't include any additional costs like *fixed assets* that you may need to buy because of the increased sales or any dividends you pay.

Growth and the way you operate your business will affect how much cash you need. Be sure you take that into account when you plan your future. Remember that as many profitable as unprofitable businesses don't make it because they run out of cash.

The ratios and interpretation of them is important to your banker so we will take a look at what they mean.

Current Ratio and Quick Ratio

A *current ratio* is defined as *Current Assets* divided by *Current Liabilities*. It tells a banker how many *current assets* are available to pay *current liabilities* and measures whether a company can meet its *current liabilities* (*accounts payable* for example) by liquidating its *current assets* (collecting *accounts receivable* or selling *inventory*). A ratio of 1:1 means you have only $1 of *current assets* for each $1 of *current liabilities* so there is no room for the slow collection of a receivable or *inventory* that won't sell. Also, each lender will tell you what *current assets* can be used in the calculation although generally, the *current assets* will be defined only as cash, *accounts receivable* and *inventory*. For My Manufacturing Ltd. the *current ratio* 1.80:1 in Year 1, 1.49:1 in Year 2 and Year 3.

Inventory is two steps away from cash because you have to sell and collect the *account receivable*. *Quick ratio* helps to determine how liquid a company is assuming it cannot sell its *inventory* in time to pay its *current liabilities* and the only *current assets* available are cash and the collection of *accounts receivable*. *Inventory* is not included. If the ratio is less than 1:1, the company has to sell *inventory* in order to pay its *current liabilities*. For My Manufacturing Ltd., the *quick ratio* is 1.12 in Year 1, 0.74:1 in Year 2 and 0.88:1 in Year 3. In order to pay all of its *current liabilities*, it needs to sell *inventory* in Year 2 and Year 3.

A higher ratio is better but what is correct for the company will, like other ratios, depend on the company itself and the industry it is in. Retailers are a great example where the *current ratio* is the same as the *quick ratio* as the majority of sales are for cash or on credit card. They don't have any *accounts receivable*, so they need to sell *inventory* to pay back the money they owe. I have a good friend who owns a ladies' clothing store and needs to purchase her *inventory* on a credit card. Times have been tough for the past three years or so and she has not been profitable. She cannot get loans from a bank so needs to pay the higher interest rate charged for credit cards. She has negotiated with her suppliers though and pays them as she can. Her negotiating chip is that they would certainly get less if the store went out of business and the *inventory* needed to be sold at fire-sale prices. She only deals with suppliers that will work with her and she has built their trust over the more than twelve years she has been in business.

Liquidity

Liquidity tells a banker whether you have enough cash to run the business. How fast can you convert your assets to cash? Can you pay your bills when they are due? If not, you are not liquid. Even if your business is profitable and you have convinced your banker to provide a loan, if you have no readily available cash and your loans are maxed out, you are not liquid. You can be profitable but have no available source of cash so don't confuse the two. A startling statistic is that as many profitable businesses fail, as unprofitable ones, simply because they run out of cash.

An electrician who was a client of the bank had a great business but had only one client. Even though his company was profitable, he didn't bother to chase his customer when the invoices were not paid on time. Unfortunately for him, his client went out of business and he never did get paid. He was relying on that cash to pay his own bills and ended up losing not only his business but declaring personal bankruptcy. The size of the client and the type of business does not matter—it is the ability to pay what is owed when it is owed that matters. In 2008, Lehman Brothers was forced into bankruptcy as it ran out of cash and could not meet its obligations. The entire banking system worldwide faced a *liquidity* crisis which was only resolved when governments provided much needed short-term loans to those considered creditworthy.

Liquidity is measured both through cash flow and an assessment of the relationship between *current assets* (those that are supposed to provide cash within a year like the receivables the electrician thought he could collect) and *current liabilities* (what you need to pay in a year).

Solvency

Solvency measures the ability to survive long term. A solvent company has more in assets than it owes, meaning it has a positive net worth or *equity*. It tells a banker how much others have invested in the company (as loans or payables, for example) for every dollar of *equity* you have. *Leverage* is the amount a company owes, or its liabilities, divided by the *equity* it has. A *leverage* ratio of 1:1 means that for every dollar the shareholders have invested in the company, others have a dollar invested. The larger the ratio, the more *leverage* a company has and the likelihood of success decreases as the ratio increases. It provides a "cushion" for lenders and defines how much the company can lose, or the assets can shrink or lose value (such as the write-off of a receivable a customer cannot pay) before the lender loses money. If a company is insolvent, it either goes out of business or the assets are sold for less than the money owed. In either case, the shareholders are the first to lose money.

In 2015, Radio Shack went bankrupt as it had assets of only $1.2 billion and debts of $1.38 billion and its stores were either sold or closed. In 2016, the holding company for the Bauer brand, Performance Sports Group had to be restructured. In that case, there were assets of $594 million and liabilities of $607 million. Both companies were insolvent. Even if they sold all their assets, they would not have been able to pay off all of the money they owed.

The common term to measure *leverage* is debt divided by *equity* (debt to *equity*) but there are variations in how it is calculated so make sure you understand what your lender is looking for. In this case, a lower ratio is better. A detailed calculation of My Manufacturing Ltd. *leverage* ratios is included in the Addendum.

Pay Principal and Interest on Debt

Lenders take *liquidity* and *solvency* into account in the decision to lend you money. The company's ability to meet debt payments is measured by a *debt service coverage ratio* (DSCR). It gives an idea of how much cash is available to make interest and scheduled *current portion of long term debt* so it tells them if you can pay interest when it is due (*liquidity*) and if you have the long term potential to repay the entire debt going forward (*solvency*). As with the *solvency* ratios, make sure you understand how it is calculated as that can vary. Typically, it is some variation on earnings before interest, taxes, *depreciation* and *amortization* (*EBITDA*) and any adjustment will depend on your business. The rule of thumb is that DSCR should be at least 1.25:1. That is the amount of cash available to pay debt payments (interest plus the *current portion of long term debt*) should be 1.25 times what the debt payments are. If you are interested, the calculation of DSCR for My Manufacturing Ltd. for Year 3 is included in the Addendum.

The ratios for My Manufacturing range from 1.3 to 1.52 depending on the calculation. Both of these ratios are strong so it tells the company and its banker that My Manufacturing should be able to pay back principal and interest. Keep in mind though that this calculation is before other uses of cash including taxes, any amount needed to buy *fixed assets*, and any dividends that are paid. Some banks will calculate "*adjusted EBITDA*" and reduce *EBITDA* by cash taxes paid, *fixed assets* you buy and dividends you pay and that's why you need to understand how they calculate the number.

Who cares?

Most negative discussions between a client and a lender happen because the borrower did not understand what he needed to do. A signature on a document means you agree to do what the bank expects you to do in order for them to provide you with a loan. If you don't understand what that is, it's pretty hard to live up to those expectations. I have had many a conversation with customers who had no idea what they had done wrong and a lot of those were about the owner taking money out of the company by paying back shareholder loans. Almost every small business person signs what is called a *guarantee* and *Postponement of Claim* and that means not only will they pay back the loan if the business can't, but they will not take money out of the company, other than salaries, without having the agreement of the bank. If you take money out of the company, not only is it breaching the agreement you signed but it will affect most of the other ratios as well. It's all about understanding what you sign. If you don't understand something, ask. You need to build rapport and trust.

Understand why your *financial statements* are as

important to you as they are to your banker. They represent a scorecard of how well you have done in the past and that is a good predictor of the future.

ADDENDUM

A cash flow analysis for My Manufacturing Ltd.:

- In Year 2, the owner needed to find $82,600 to finance the operating cycle. (Receivables of $89,600 plus *inventory* of $93,500 less payables of $100,500).
- Sales in Year 3 increased by $13,000 or 15.8% (Sales in Year 3 of $951,600 less sales of $821,600 in Year 2 equals $13,000. $13,000 divided by sales in Year 2 of $821,600 equals 15.8%). Using the rule of thumb that receivables, *inventory* and payables increase a similar amount to sales, the amount needed to finance the operating cycle would have been $95,650 (receivables of $103,756 plus *inventory* of $108,273 less payables of $116,379) calculated as follows:

    —Receivables would have increased to approximately $103,756 (last year's balance of $89,600 plus 15.8%),

    —*Inventory* to approximately $108,273 (last year's balance of $93,500 plus 15.8%)

—Payables to approximately $116,379 (last year's balance of $100,500 plus 15.8%).

The amount of cash required would have increased $13,050 from the year before ($95,650 less $82,600) simply because sales grew.

It was actually $91,800 (receivables of $116,000 plus *inventory* of $91,800 less payables of $105,900) as the owner did something differently. The company collected receivables slower (the balance was $116,000 instead of $103,756 had he collected in the same time), *inventory* sold faster (the balance was only $91,800 instead of $108,273 had he done business the same way) but the suppliers were paid more quickly (the balance was only $105,900 compared to $116,379).

All in all, the company needed to come up with $18,600 to finance his operating cycle—$13,050 because of the growth he experienced and the balance of $5,550 because he did not run his business the same way. That doesn't include any other costs like an increase in *fixed assets* that may be required as a result of the sales increase.

Solvency ratio calculations for My Manufacturing Ltd.:
- Debt to *equity* in its simplest form considers debt as borrowed money so it does not include things like payables. For My Manufacturing

Ltd., in Year 3 debt to *equity* is 4.98:1 (debt of $274,500 divided by *equity* of $55,100). That means for every dollar the owner has in *equity*, other lenders have almost $5.
- Total liabilities to *equity* is a variation so includes all money that is owed by the company like *accounts payable*. For My Manufacturing Ltd., total liabilities to *equity* is 7.12:1 (total liabilities of $392,100 divided by *equity* of $55,100). For every dollar of *equity*, others are owed over $7.
- Due to shareholders can be considered *equity* if the shareholder has agreed in writing not to take the money out of the company. If the shareholder for My Manufacturing Ltd. agrees to that, in Year 3, the shareholder is owed $19,600 so that amount is deducted from debt and added to *equity*. On that basis debt to *equity* is 3.41:1 (debt of $254,900 divided by *equity* of $74,700) and total liabilities to *equity* is 4.99:1 (debt of $372,500 divided by *equity* of $74,700).

DSCR calculations for My Manufacturing Ltd.:
- Results from the previous year are built into the formula so interest and principal payments actually paid last year are calculated to provide the debt service. For example, using the

financial statements of My Manufacturing Ltd., *EBITDA* in Year 3 is $51,100 (earnings before interest and taxes of $44,100 plus $7,000 of *depreciation*), interest is $19,500 and scheduled principal payments last year were $13,900 (*current portion of long term debt* from Year 2). DSCR is 1.52 ($51,100 divided by ($19,500 + 13,900).

- If debt is increasing or the business is changing, the new debt is added in. In the case of My Manufacturing Ltd., debt payments due next year are $16,500 (*current portion of long term debt* from Year 3) and interest next year is projected to be $22,600. DSCR for Year 4 is about 1.30:1 based on *EBITDA* for Year 3 ($51,100 divided by $16,500 plus $22,600). This does not include any increase in *EBITDA* that may be realized so the actual ratio may be higher.

Chapter 4

The Five "Cs" of Credit and Loan Pricing

When my job was to approve loans, I met with a new client who had been in the manufacturing industry for a long time. It was clear he felt I had no right to ask questions even though he had applied for a loan of more than $25 million. When I met him in his boardroom, I was dressed like a banker in a suit and heels but it was evident from his reaction that I was not at all what he expected. I was probably twenty-five years younger than he was, short, and a woman. He was impatient and it showed in his answers to my questions. At one point, he asked me sarcastically how many more questions I needed to ask. I could almost picture him rolling his eyes. My response was simple. I would ask as many as I needed to understand his business and decide if I was prepared to sign off on his application. I added that I hoped if he were lending that much money to someone he'd be just as diligent. Fortunately, that did the trick and he answered unhesitatingly after that.

To comprehend why the barrage of questions seems unrelenting when you apply for a loan, it is important to understand the system. The processes in most banks are similar. The person you meet with initially is usually called an account manager and has some knowledge of your industry. He asks some questions. Your request then likely goes to someone else to analyze your *financial statements* and write the credit application. That may generate other questions. Depending on the amount of the loan, and this does differ from bank to bank, the request will go to someone who can either approve the loan or needs to recommend the loan to someone who has the authority to approve it. That person may have more questions as might the person who has to approve the loan. So by the end of it, you have answered questions from at least three different people who likely all have a different level of understanding of your industry and your business. The better they understand it, the better off you are.

Early one Monday morning, I was in my office on the top floor of the building enjoying the sight of the sun hitting the snow on the mountains. I received two urgent applications that needed quick responses. Both were for more than $25 million and were a bid situation—the clients had gone to more than one bank and whoever answered first with the best deal won the business and the right to negotiate the deal. Both had a drop-dead date and came from the same business centre but different account managers. The clients needed the money so they could remove the *"subject to financing"* clause in their bid before a set date. That happened often when I was in the credit department and responsible for approving loans or "working them up" for others to sign. The centre manager ran the business and had about ten account managers reporting to him. He had to let me know which deal was the most urgent. I couldn't do both at the same time.

Imagine you are the center manager in a situation like this. Two customers need a loan and both have firm deadlines. You have to decide which to pursue first and risk losing the business of the other. Both are in the tight-knit oil and gas industry so it is unlikely what you decide won't become common knowledge. One client always does what he commits to and makes sure he explains what he is doing and where he is going. The other client is always late with payments, never provides information on time, needs to be pushed to discuss his plans and continually surprises by doing things he hasn't mentioned. When both are good clients, the choice is a difficult one but when there is a difference between the two it is easy.

And it's just as easy for you to decide what kind of client to be. If you are a good client, most bankers will go to any lengths to make sure your needs are met.

When I was an account manager, I received a call from an investment banker one morning at about 6 o'clock before the stock market opened. I had less than thirty minutes to respond to a request that would generate in excess of $200,000 for the bank and we were competing with several other banks. We had to respond before the market opened. I called Fred in the credit department who was responsible for making the decision but he was in a meeting and would need to call me back. I waited as long as I could and called again but to no avail. I wondered if it was worth my job to make him angry and decided it was.

Because it was an internal meeting, I had him interrupted to make my case and as I suspected he was furious. I called the chief risk officer and within five minutes the deal was approved. He said he didn't have the authority to approve the request but would take the chance. I responded that if he didn't have that authority, I clearly didn't but if he didn't approve it I would do it anyway. We won the business. That is an extreme example of the ends bankers will go to for good clients. This happened to be for a large amount of money, but it does happen at all levels. Fred became my boss not too long after but neither of us spoke of the confrontation again.

An important part of knowing customers and being able to help them is to understand their industry's risks and challenges. When I was an account manager, we were generalists and handled any client who walked through the door. We found out what they wanted and what the business did when we asked. Now banks have a screening process that makes sure there is a match between the client and the account manager.

The first and only time I managed an airline was a huge learning experience. As is the case with any industry, it has unique characteristics but it happens to be one of the riskiest. All you need to do is look back in history to understand the number of airlines that have been bought by others or simply gone out of business. When was the last time you flew Canadian, Wardair, PanAm, or TWA? During a meeting when the airline was having some cash flow problems, the President and Chief Executive Officer said, "Folks fall in love with the romance of the industry." He knew the risks in the business and was sharing what most people don't until it is too late. The big problem then, as now, is few know how to run a profitable business by flying airplanes.

And before there were specialists, few bankers knew how to lend to one. I had to learn about the airline industry and how to lend to it. At that time, there were only two large airlines in Canada and not long after I changed jobs, one bought the other. Since then, one large and several regional carriers have popped up so more bankers are exposed to the industry. Now I fly a lot and only recently found out you had to pay for a blanket if it is cold on the airplane. Travellers are paying for anything extra to help increase revenues.

I had clients who were paranoid if I also managed their competitors' accounts. I once banked two publicly traded electrical providers and was terrified that I would get the names wrong and give them reason to be uneasy. Bankers now claim to provide financial advice, like how much and what kind of loans are appropriate and they need knowledge of the industry and the business to do that. Almost all lenders have specialists that deal with a particular industry and related businesses—be it supply chain, professionals, not-for-profit, etc. An account manager who specializes in transportation today would manage any airline account in his geography and could reach out to others managing the same industry elsewhere if questions arose. The idea is that each client benefits from the expertise the banker has and adds to it.

Providing advice is now a competitive advantage. Most bankers are paid for increasing business and while there are other products, for small business the primary one is money. If you cannot get a loan from a bank, it is highly unlikely you will buy other products from it. Understanding the industry is paramount when providing advice and money.

Some types of business are risky by their nature as I found out with the airline. Industry risks are the same for everyone involved and knowing what to focus on will help you run your business. As an example, restaurants face numerous challenges that other businesses do not. Predicting sales and purchasing *inventory* are important success factors in every retail business but for a restaurant what you don't sell within a tight window goes bad and has no salvage value. Contrast that to a clothing store that may have *inventory* that loses value over the season if its stock goes out of fashion but it will likely be still worth something. End-of-season sales markdown prices of goods like bathing suits but still generate cash.

Think about a seasonal business that manufactures snow shovels. If there is no snow, the shovels likely won't sell and the manufacturer will not be able to generate any cash. The end result of the analysis is what lenders call an *industry risk rating* (IRR) and becomes part of the overall rating of your loan. Usually, that rating is provided to the account manager as the IRR is determined by an economics department and is judged based on relative industries.

To help decide which clients to pursue and which ones to pass on, a lender learns the five "Cs" of credit: *character*, *capacity*, *collateral*, *conditions* and *capital*. Borrowers need to understand and pay attention to them. Over the years, it has become the formula to get to know customers, figure out what makes them tick, and what is important to each.

The first and most important "C" is *character*. It is not negotiable. If you can't pass that hurdle, the others don't matter. If your *character* is good, the other "Cs" become important and will be assessed but you can trade off elements of one for the other. Almost every loan is a bit different depending on what is important to the borrower and the bank. I tell my students to try to figure out what the hot buttons are for their clients. For example, small businesses do not like to pay fees but don't mind paying a bit more interest. Publicly traded companies don't mind paying fees but want the lowest interest rate possible. Knowing what is important lets both sides win.

Character

Niel is a self-employed general contractor. He's been in business for eight years, incorporated for three, and his specialty is flooring. He is proud of his work and was invited to bid on our floors when we did renovations. Niel acknowledged that one of the biggest risks in the contracting industry is the lack of certification and folks attempting to do things they are not qualified for. He found out the hard way when he first started his business and decided to wire his own house with what he referred to as a library book on the 1-2-3's of electrical. The bad news was that he wired his stove for 110 volts instead of 220 so the clock worked but the burners didn't. The good news was that he didn't burn his house down. He now hires "masters," to do anything but flooring.

Niel used to drive a large yellow diesel truck with a box that he bought when he moved to Calgary from Hull in 2008. His uncle won the lottery and gave him enough money so that he didn't need a loan for the truck. He credited his success to folks who helped him out along the way and he believed in karma and giving back. He had a tattoo of the love of his life, Liz, on his arm, had a wallet in his pocket attached to a chain on his belt that is full of receipts, and played his boom box when he worked. While he ran his operation like it was a multi-million-dollar company, he had never thought about how he could leverage his business with a bank loan and save himself cash.

Niel stood by his work. He has kept in touch and two years after he laid the floor in the living room, he spent two days on his own nickel to fix some problems. That speaks huge volumes about how he values his reputation. He has stuck his neck out to help others in the past and has been badly burned but continues to help whoever he can.

Most banks have a rule that they will not lend money to someone who had previous loans written off but that is too black and white. Many small businesses fail for reasons the owner can't control like an economic slump or a change in the neighbourhood. In the early days of lending to high technology companies, we banked a small firm that had a great product. In order to save money, it outsourced the manufacturing to an overseas plant. One day, the folks in that plant stopped returning phone calls and supplying products. Our clients had no recourse when they couldn't meet payroll. They went out of business and we wrote off the loan. Perhaps they should have done more due diligence or had one of their own employees in the plant but that might not have changed the ending.

My friend has a ladies' clothing store and sales have dropped significantly through no fault of her own. The City decided to build a homeless shelter not far from her location, a methadone clinic opened around the corner from the shop, and the road was closed for construction. All of these may have a positive impact on society but may not generate the kind of traffic she needs to build her sales. She is managing to stay alive but is faced with challenges she has no control over. It would be unfair to lump all of the blame on her if the store fails. It is more about how the owner reacts to the failure than the fact the business fails.

I once had a call from an account manager looking at lending money to a company but we had previously written off debt for one of the shareholders. The question I asked him, and what I tell my students to ask when confronted with a similar situation, is, "What did the owner do when things went wrong?" A client who throws the keys across the desk and expects the banker to clean up the mess is quite different than one who takes accountability and works with the bank to help minimize losses. In this case, the client did everything possible to help the situation. We had no problem with his *character* and ended up recommending the loan and it got approved. Had he made it the bank's problem and not worked with us to maximize collections, I have no doubt the outcome would have been quite different.

Financial statements are a scorecard of what has happened in the business. I once was asked if I would consider including income that was not included in the reports as part of the loan payment. To reduce taxes, the client did not declare sales if customers paid in cash. Sound familiar? That is dishonest and I would not even think about providing a loan to someone like that, even if we didn't need the cash income to justify the loan. It goes back to *character*; that is non-negotiable. He was dishonest so the rest of the "Cs" don't count.

A personal *credit bureau* score is part of the *character* assessment as small business owners will generally handle their personal and company debts the same way. Scores are affected by many things, including the number of credit enquiries. If you are shopping around for financing, ask your lender to do a soft *credit bureau*, which doesn't affect your credit rating. It tells the lender what your *credit score* is before the debt you are requesting is added. If you are approved, then a complete or hard *credit bureau* can be done and that *credit score* takes into account the new debt. A *credit score* is negatively affected by the number of hard checks—the number of times you are requesting credit. A soft check will not affect your score as it does not add in the debt you might apply for.

Niel and Liz own two houses and they financed 75 percent of the purchase prices so they did not have to pay the extra fee to have the mortgages insured by Canada Mortgage and Housing Corporation. They managed to come up with the required down payments through family loans. Liz was going to school in a different city but has since graduated and found employment in that city. She and Niel commute whenever they can to see each other. He lives in the basement bedroom of one house and she lives in the attic of the other while she went to school and continues to do so. They rent the rest of both houses to make sure they have sufficient cash to meet the mortgage payments and have never missed one. Niel tells me he had a bad credit rating before he moved to Calgary several years back but it is now a good risk with a *credit score* of 680. That goes to prove that a change in attitude and behaviour can have an impact on your creditworthiness.

Niel is making sure that when he decides to go to a bank for a loan for his company, his *character* will be an asset, not a liability. If the *character* hurdle is not met, any other information will be moot.

Capacity

Years ago, one of my neighbours borrowed over $25 million for his business in the oil and gas services industry. When business slumped because of an overall downturn in the economy and he couldn't pay it back, he went to the local newspaper and blamed the bank for lending him too much money. Nobody leaves my classroom thinking the correct answer to how much you need is as much as you will give me.

Capacity in this context means the maximum loans that the business can repay over a specified time. The *Office of the Superintendent of Financial Institutions* (OSFI) regulates all institutions in Canada that lend money and one of the regulations is that each loan is reviewed at least annually. The *capacity* of a business can change year to year. The purpose of the loan determines what the "specified time period" will be and whether the loan is revolving or reducing.

A revolving loan is similar to a credit card as it is used to fund temporary cash needs. For example, you charge *inventory* and repay the amount when the *inventory* is sold and paid for. You pay interest only on the amount of the loan outstanding and are not expected to make scheduled payments as the loan "revolves" or pays down by any cash received. The interest rate on a loan is much lower than a credit card, which is typically between 19 and 25 percent if you don't pay your balance off monthly. If you pay the entire balance monthly it costs you no interest.

Niel uses only a credit card with a limit of $10,000 and often carries a balance as he does not have a revolving loan. If he doesn't pay off the $10,000, his interest charge for a year would be over $3,000. If he had a revolving loan it would probably cost him about 5 percent or $500 a year. Once his *financial statements* are finalized this year, and he has his *business plan* developed, we'll see if the bank will provide him with a revolving loan. He can then use his credit card without paying any interest for thirty days and pay it off fully using his revolving loan. He has a proven credit history with his credit card as he has never missed a payment and by saving that much interest each year he should qualify to borrow at least $10,000 so he doesn't have to carry the balance over.

If the loan is to purchase an asset like a truck, the period will be slightly less than the expected life of the truck or about seven years. If it is to purchase land and buildings, the period can be as long as twenty-five years. These are reducing loans and you pay back the principal plus interest by making scheduled payments (the *current portion of long term debt* including *interest* or plus *interest*). I once reviewed a file that the "specified time period" was twenty-five years and the loan was for a truck. I get it that it was secured by land but the truck would need to be replaced long before the twenty-five years and the loan would never be repaid. Every time a new truck had to be purchased, the loan just increased.

You need to show the banker that your company can generate enough cash over and above what it costs to run the business to meet interest and any scheduled principal payments. In a prior chapter, we talked about the *Debt Service Coverage Ratio* (DSCR) and that it generally needs to be at least 1.25. That means for every dollar you need to pay for principal and interest, your business has $1.25 of cash left over after all expenses of the business have been met. If you are already in business, most bankers will want to see at least three years of *financial statements* to determine *"sustainable" cash flow*. If you are just starting up, *projections* will be the starting point. If the business is your only paycheck, make sure you budget to pay yourself enough to make your personal loan payments. In Niel and Liz's case, the money from renting the two houses meets the mortgage payments but Niel has a car loan the company has to repay.

Debt is a tool that can help a business grow, but too much can destroy it. Don't lose sight of the fact that at some point you need to repay it. You need to think of it in the same way you think about personal debt. Most of us rely on debt for specific things, such as buying a house, but are happy when we can repay it. That's maybe why there are mortgage-burning parties. The same thing should apply to your business.

Collateral

When I started lending money, I financed an ice cream parlour in a small town and it was doing quite well. Frank, the owner, was a rotund Italian who had eaten more than his share of rich desserts. He had been in Canada for only a short time and was proud of his business. I visited the parlour, sampled all his flavours of ice cream and washed them down with a cappuccino. Stomach ache notwithstanding, it was delicious.

Then, Frank decided to open a second location. I declined the loan. I explained to him that I believed the town was too small and his focus should stay on his existing business until it was firmly established. Ice cream doesn't make great *security* and the business was seasonal—more lucrative during the hot summer than during the winter and where he was located, there were definitely four seasons. He accepted a loan from another bank, using his home as *collateral*. I was not happy to be right this time but as I suspected neither location was successful because Frank couldn't be at both places at once and had borrowed too much money. The bank was forced to *foreclose* and he not only lost his businesses but also his house.

Collateral is also called *security* and will be sold to pay off your loans if the business cannot. It is a second way out, or secondary source of repayment. Most lenders in Canada will have you sign a *General Security Agreement* and register it under the *Personal Property Security Act*. A similar system operates in Quebec but it is referred to differently. Whichever province you are in, the document gives them *security* on anything in the business that is not real estate and includes assets like *accounts receivables*, *inventory*, and things like trucks that are identified by serial numbers. Real estate, like your house mortgage, will be a different document and registered at the *Land Titles Office*. If you do not live up to your commitments, the lender has to give you proper legal notice (which is currently set at ten days) but can take possession of the *security* and sell the assets to pay off loans.

Many small businesses do not own sufficient assets to provide *security* for loans and owners will need to sign a personal *guarantee*, which means that if the business fails, you agree to personally make sure all loans are paid off. The bank can sue you at the same time it takes possession of the business assets and does not have to wait until those are sold.

Be sure to understand what you are providing for *collateral*. In my early years, I approved a loan to a tech start-up provided the *security* included the proprietary technology it had developed. The owner said no and because I couldn't understand the rationale, I asked the account manager to ask more questions. It turned out that the revenues and cash flow depended on licensing the technology to clients and the owner believed our *security* would preclude that. Once she realized our *security* would not interfere with her business, she had no problem signing the documents. The company is still successful today.

As an owner, you need to stand by your business, be prepared to take calculated risks but also take advice to heart. You might not always agree, but at least listen and think about it. Don't be afraid to provide *collateral* but understand what it means. If Frank had listened to advice early on, over time he probably would have had two ice cream parlours and his house.

Conditions

My main *security* for the airline I lent to was airplanes that flew all over the world. If something happened and the airline stopped flying, my concern was that I wouldn't be able to track down my *security* to sell and pay back loans. We put a condition in our agreement that the company had to agree to fly the planes to an agreed-upon place if something went wrong. They knew where they were and had crew on the ground with them. We would have to pay for the return of the airplanes but at least we would know where they were. Make sure you think it through, though. Where would I put all of those airplanes?

Conditions are the rules. They spell out what both the lender and the borrower can and can't do. Unfortunately, a lot of business owners are in such a hurry to get money and so relieved, they don't take the time to understand what they are signing. Little wonder they are surprised when the bank tells them they are in "*default*," meaning they did not do what they signed on for.

Most business loans are *demand loans*. The lender can ask to be paid back at any time without providing a reason as long as the borrower is given the legally defined time to do so. If the loans are revolving, it is at the bank's discretion to provide further funds even if you have not borrowed all that was offered. Missed payments are the most common reason to *demand loans*, but not the only reason.

A lender that didn't understand the concept of *demand loans* went a little too far a few years back. A retail store closed down and papered the windows but the lender did not demand as long as the owner made payments. The purpose of the loan was to run a retail shop and that wasn't happening so eventually the lender demanded. The owner had continued to pay rent and that depleted the amount that was available to pay back the loans. Had the lender demanded loans as soon as the company closed down, the loss would have been less. And a taxi business we lent to expanded the business to include other activities that we suspected were against the law and criminal. The loans were not used for the purpose described in our offer, to operate a taxi business and not acceptable to the bank. We asked the customer to find another bank and pay us off within ten days and we did not need to give him a reason. Our only evidence was credit card receipts and while we would have had a problem proving our suspicions, we did not need to. I suspect he knew and refinanced the business as a taxi somewhere else.

The best protection is to ask your lender to explain any document you sign to make sure you understand and agree to it. Some *conditions* are negotiable and some are not. I like to compare a negotiation to a football game. Both sides know where their goalposts are and those are the things that are not negotiable. Everything else is a compromise. My negotiation style was always to give in on anything I didn't need to backstop the loan. If the borrower doesn't do the same thing when the negotiation is ending, he will offer to give me something in return for something I give him. If I have nothing left to give, he has lost his opportunity to compromise and trade off terms and *conditions*. I had that happen once. The deal was for a loan in excess of $200 million and meetings went on for months. Throughout the negotiation, I provided concessions at any point I could and the customer held back on some issues that he hoped to trade off at the end. Just before we signed the deal, he raised his remaining issues but had no bargaining power as I had already agreed to everything I could. He had not negotiated well. He was accustomed to trade-offs in past negotiations and didn't understand my style was different. Know what you need and make sure your lender knows it, too.

For any size of loan, a non-negotiable condition is the provision of *financial statements* within a stipulated time. How often you need to provide them is negotiable so if it is more frequently than annually, ask why. If you understand what the lender needs, you may be able to provide it some other way that is easier and less expensive for you and suitable for them. Often your lender just needs to have a look at a listing of receivables, *inventory* and payables monthly, so you may be able to just provide those and not full financials.

The *conditions*, including how often you have to provide *financial statements*, are a function of how risky the loan is. A company with a long history of *profits* and success, together with an owner who leaves money in the business to help fund the operations will face fewer *conditions* than a start-up with no proven track record or an owner who pays every cent the company makes out to shareholders. Most businesses fall somewhere in the middle so negotiating *conditions* both parties feel are fair is important.

Capital

Many years ago, I consulted with a profitable small company but Jamie, the owner, took a lot of money out of it. He had the business and his personal accounts linked at the bank so the money was simply transferred from the corporate account if he needed money. He drew so much to meet his lifestyle that the company could not pay its employees and the bank threatened to *demand loans*. The amount the company could borrow, or its *capacity*, was overshadowed by the fact that the shareholder was taking too much money out of the company and that amount was not available to run the company or pay back loans. As a small business person, you need to understand what cash is available to pay back the bank. If you take it out, it is not.

I met with the lender, had the accounts unlinked and took away his access to the business cash. Jamie and his wife showed up at a meeting with the staff that had not been paid. She was dressed in a green silk dress and fur coat and wanted to know when she could start spending money again. We managed to save the company after the owners agreed to go on a budget and stop draining the company. It is still in business and recently sold to a larger firm.

Capital is the amount of money the owner or owners have put into the business. It includes any cash invested originally or after start-up and any money the company made that was not paid out to the shareholders. It also considers whether the owners have cash outside of the business that can be used if needed to fund the ongoing operations. The consulting company owner may have put a lot of *capital* in the business but his lifestyle led him to take too much out.

The more cash in the business the less the risk you won't be able to pay loans back. If you have purchased a camper truck, an off-road vehicle and gone on vacations all at the expense of the business, that is not considered *capital* of the business as none of those add value to its operation. They are also a drain on cash. Remember that on a *balance sheet*, assets equal liabilities plus owners' *equity*. Unless an asset is purchased for use in the business, like a piece of land for future expansion, it is subtracted from the *equity* of the business. Also, any amount you invested in new technology might be subtracted from *equity* until the value of the innovation is proven.

You need to keep your business separate from your personal lifestyle. Any money you take out of cash flow decreases the amount left to pay expenses, including repaying the bank. If possible, it doesn't hurt to have an emergency stash of cash for the business as you do in your personal life. It is true that if you put all of your money into your business, it shows that you support it. On the other hand, if you do that and unexpected expenses come up, you may have no access to *capital*.

The 5 "Cs" and Pricing

Few lenders will agree to provide money if you don't have the right *character* but the other "Cs" are not as etched in stone. Different *conditions* can put you in the same place as long as both sides are prepared to compromise.

The end result of assessing the five "Cs" is what is commonly called a risk rating. Most financial institutions have their own computer models and what you pay for loans is linked to where that number falls out. The better the risk rating, the lower the interest rate you pay. If you are not happy with the pricing on your loan, ask what you need to do to improve it. Typically, as the financial strength of your company improves, so does your pricing. Most loans are priced at prime plus a *spread* that can vary from zero to about five percent, depending on the institution.

The cost of writing off loans is high and protecting shareholders' money is part of a lender's job. If the bank has a cost of funds (what it pays to depositors) of three percent and lends $100,000 out for five percent, it nets only $2,000 in interest for a full year. That has to pay for staff, overhead expenses and generate a *profit*. If that $100,000 is written off, the bank has to make $5,000,000 of loans at five percent for a whole year to make up for that write off of the principal and that doesn't cover the time or cost of trying to collect the loan. That helps to explain why there are so many questions and it can take so long to get money approved. What seems to be expensive to a small business owner is actually a good deal.

You are your business and need to understand what is important to a lender. If there is a history behind any of the 5 "Cs," be open and honest. Explain what happened upfront. If your lender is surprised to find out something you haven't told him, it affects your credibility and your *character*. That is not negotiable.

Chapter 5

What Options Are There for Financing and What Are You Agreeing To?

Niel started his flooring business in 2008 in Hull and moved to Calgary in 2011. He initially used a credit card to finance his business. He charged everything he used on it—from paint to flooring and everything in-between. The interest rate was a business one so lower than a personal rate but he did not have sufficient cash to pay it off monthly. His interest costs were between $3,000 and $5,000 over the years. On revenues of about $200,000 or less, that adds up. It probably was a good idea when he started out as I suspect without a history and minimal net worth, he would have had problems getting a loan. Now that he's established though, it is an expensive way to do business.

So what is the best form of financing for your business? There are several options available and each has a specific purpose and interest rates and other terms and *conditions* vary. It may seem overwhelming at first but it's really no different than buying a car. You speak to friends to get their advice and shop for the one that suits you best. Each model has unique features that affect the cost and then it all comes down to a trade-off. Do you want to pay for the supercharged version or not? Negotiating a loan is no different. You need to match what you need to the appropriate product. Talk to an accountant to help you determine what best suits your requirements. Then, talk to more than one banker to better understand what each is offering. Be persistent and make sure you understand what the overall deal looks like.

Basic Offerings

Let's explore the various types of what we'll call *"conventional" financing*—that is financing provided by your bank. While some of these may not look like a loan, each option is a way to finance your business and as such is considered money you owe the bank (something they refer to as credit risk). Each bank has rules as to the minimum amount of loans that qualify for each type of financing. They are not all the same, so you need to shop around.

Most small businesses start with an *overdraft* or an *operating loan* to finance their basic operations, so we'll start with those and then explore the types of financing you can get to buy assets and build your business further.

Overdrafts

We are all familiar with the age-old *overdraft*, which simply says your bank will honour cheques or debits to an agreed upon amount even if you don't have money in your account. We have a small *overdraft* for our business, which helps us manage the cash flow if a deposit is late or I forget to transfer funds to the right account. We pay interest of five percent over prime and five dollars for each cheque we write when the account is overdrawn.

Usually, the bank will determine an *overdraft* limit when you apply as well as monthly interest and chequing fees. Borrowing by way of *overdraft* is normally more expensive than other types of financing but it can be a convenient and easy way to borrow if you don't need a lot of money or very often as is the case with our business. It is generally not secured which, in banking terms, means that the bank must rely on the operation of the business to repay the *overdraft*. *Overdrafts* are priced at prime plus a percentage, so rates are always variable. As prime goes up or down, so will the interest rate.

Credit Cards

Credit cards are similar to *overdrafts* in that they offer a simple way to cover immediate expenses, but they come with a cost. Rates are high and if you don't pay off the entire balance every month the interest that is owed gets added to the amount you didn't pay. So the next month you'll pay interest on the balance from the previous month along with any charges for the current month. You pay interest on what you charged and the interest you didn't pay. It is what is known as compound interest.

I was shocked to learn that the estimated time for repayment on my credit card balance of $485.92 using the minimum $10 per month was seven years. The interest rate was 19.70%. Most business credit cards have a lower interest rate but it is still an expensive way to pay your bills. On the other hand, if you pay it off in full each month, you get free money for thirty days (or whatever the *billing cycle* is).

Shopping for a credit card for a business is no different than shopping for a personal credit card. It depends if you want to build points, pay less interest, get cash back, pay an annual fee, charge in U.S. dollars—and the list goes on and on. Some banks offer "sales" for a limited time but once that "limited time" is up, standard terms and *conditions* will apply. I just got an offer in the mail that charges 7.99% for the first six months, then 19.99% for purchases and 22.99% for cash advances. The terms state that if I miss making two minimum payments in a year those rates increase to 24.99% (from 19.99) and 27.99% (from 22.99).

That means if you miss two minimum payments in a year, the increase in percentage rate charged alone translates to $3 a year for every $100 you cannot pay and that does not account for the compounding we discussed earlier. Make sure you read the small print.

The reasons to have a credit card for business vary—from keeping business expenses separate from personal ones to establishing a credit record for the business. Keep in mind that while a credit card is in the company name, in most cases it is also in your name, which means if the business cannot pay it back, you will have to. Many start-up small businesses use a credit card because they are easy to get and often the only type of financing that is readily available.

In Niel's case, the credit card was a reasonable way to finance his business for short-term costs. But, if his cash flow came up short and he couldn't pay his monthly bill, the interest was much higher than it would have been for an *overdraft* or an operating line. As an example, a credit card would be about 20%, an *overdraft* of prime plus 5% and an operating line of prime plus 2% to prime plus 3%.

Operating Loans

The most common type of loan is called an *operating loan* or a *revolving line of credit*. You use the loan when you need it to finance day-to-day operations and pay down the amount you owe with any cash you collect.

Here we will talk about what *operating loans* are best for, why it is important to understand the terms of your *operating loan*, whether you should have your loan in Canadian and U.S. dollars, and tips to impress your banker on how you manage operating accounts.

What Are They Best For?

Operating loans are used to finance your *cash cycle*, which means just what it says—from cash to cash. The *cash cycle* in our store was the time it took to buy *inventory* and pay for it and then sell it and collect any money that was owed to us. For example, if we purchased a dozen bottles of olive oil and paid for them in thirty days, but didn't sell any of them for six months, the *cash cycle* of the bottles would be five months (the six months it took to sell, less the month we had to pay for it).

A manufacturer's *cash cycle* is typically longer than a retailer's. They usually buy *raw materials* on account, and then have to make the goods and collect the payments. Otherwise, it works the same way. They pay down the *operating loan* when they sell the product.

An *operating loan* makes sense when there is a *timing difference* between when you have to pay out cash for *inventory* and when you can sell it and collect the money. Most *operating loans* have a *revolving feature*, either one-way or two-way. Two-way means that loans up to your lending limit are automatically placed in the account if you are overdrawn and any excess cash is taken out of the account to pay down your loans. Loans and payments are typically at a minimum amount say $5,000, so at times you may have cash in your account up to that amount. For example, if your account is overdrawn by $3,000, the bank will put $5,000 in your account. You will pay interest on the entire $5,000 even though $2,000 is still in your account. Conversely, if you have $6,500 in your account, your loan will only be paid down by $5,000 and the $1,500 will stay in your account. In one-way, only the first half of the transaction is automatic. That is, loans will be automatically put in your account if you are overdrawn but you have to instruct the bank to pay down your loan if you have excess funds in your account. Otherwise, you will be paying loan interest on the cash in your account that should have been used to pay down your loans.

Interest

In most cases, you pay interest only on the amount of the *revolving loan* you use although sometimes you will pay a small percentage (say ½ percent) on the part you don't use. The calculations are done daily and the interest is charged to your account on a specific day each month. Canadian dollar loans are priced at a rate above the *Prime Rate of interest* and U.S. loans are charged at a rate above the *United States Base Rate* (USBR) of interest. The amount above Prime Rate or USBR is quoted in interest rates and the interest rate you pay above that rate is called a *spread*. For example, if the interest rate on your loan is Prime plus two percent, and Prime Rate is four percent, you will pay six percent. The amount you pay above Prime or USBR is negotiated between you and your banker. Prime Rate and USBR are the same for every borrower and change with market conditions. You will be notified by the bank if the rate changes as that will change the amount of interest you pay. Prime Rate is normally based on the *Bank of Canada Rate of Interest,* and USBR on the Federal Reserve Board Prime Rate in the U.S.

US Dollars

If you buy *inventory* and have receivables in U.S. dollars, you can often have part of your *operating loan* in U.S. dollars so you do not have to convert to Canadian every time you make or receive a payment in U.S. dollars. See example below:

Say you receive U.S. $1,000 from a customer. When your bank converts that to Canadian dollars it uses the current exchange rate plus it charges you a bit extra. If that rate is 83 cents, you will receive $1,205 in Canadian dollars (U.S. $1,000 divided by 83 cents). If you have to pay U.S. $1,000 for products from the U.S. and the rate has changed to 80 cents then it will cost you $1,250 (U.S. $1,000 divided by 80 cents). The two conversions cost you $45. If you had a U.S. *operating loan*, the U.S. $1,000 would be U.S. $1,000 and you would not pay the cost of conversion nor suffer losses because the Canadian dollar was worth less. If you sell and buy in U.S. dollars infrequently it may not be worth having the option to borrow in U.S. but if not it may be worth your while to look into it.

Margins

Depending on the financial institution and the amount of your loans, at some point, it might be a term of your *operating loan* that the amount you can borrow is managed through a formula called a margin.

You will be required to submit a report to the bank, either monthly or quarterly depending on how often your loan is margined, usually on the 20th of the month. In it, you will detail any *accounts receivable* you have and how old they are (usually referred to as an *aged listing of accounts receivable*) and the value at cost of your *inventory*. The amount you can borrow is determined by the last report you submitted. The margin formula varies with the financial institution and the amount of your loans and details, and the form for the report, are detailed in the documents you signed when you agreed to the terms of the loan.

To use a simplified example, if the last report showed *accounts receivable* of $120,000 and *inventory* of $100,000 and the margin formula is 75 percent of receivables and 50 percent of *inventory*, you would be able to borrow up to $130,000 (75 percent of $120,000 plus 50 percent of $100,000). While an overall limit is set when you apply the amount you can borrow is limited by this formula. In this example, your *operating loan* would be approved up to the lesser of the margin amount and a set amount, say $200,000. Based on the calculation, you would only be able to borrow $130,000. If at the time the report is given to the bank you are actually borrowing $150,000, you have to pay back $20,000 to bring your loan back down to $130,000.

Let's look at the terminology that is common for an *operating loan* that is limited by a margining formula. A description might say that loans are limited to the lesser of the amount approved and the sum of 75 percent of *eligible accounts receivable* and 50 percent of *inventory*, less *priority claims*.

Your banker will give you a definition of these terms but an *eligible account receivable* is usually any *account receivable* that is under ninety days old. If it is over ninety days old, your customer has not paid you for over ninety days from the invoice date. If more than a set percentage of the total the client owes you, normally 10 percent is over ninety days old then the entire receivable must be removed from your margin.

As an example, if one of your customers owes you $10,000 and has not paid you for ninety-five days, the $10,000 cannot be included as part of your margining formula. If you have total receivables of $120,000, you have to take this $10,000 off. You can only borrow up to 75% of $110,000. Instead of being able to borrow $90,000, you can only borrow $85,000. If only $500 is ninety-five days old, because the amount is less than 10% only $500 will be taken off of your total receivables and you will be able to borrow $89,625 ($120,000 less $500 times 75%).

Priority claims are any amounts that have the legal right to be paid to someone else before the bank is paid. These amounts are deducted from the margin value of the loan.

As an example, say you owe the government $15,000 for payroll deductions like Canada Pension, Employment Insurance, or Incomes Taxes you have taken off the paycheques of employees. Because the government must be paid before the bank loan is repaid, these are considered *priority claims* and reduce the amount of loans that are available to you. In this example, if your margin formula says you can borrow $100,000 but you owe the Government $15,000, you will only be able to borrow $85,000.

If at the end of the month your *eligible accounts receivable* are $200,000, *inventory* is $250,000, and *priority claims* are $50,000, you can only borrow $225,000 (75% of $200,000 plus 50% of $250,000 or $275,000 less $50,000).

Other examples of payments that might be *priority claims*:

- Federal or provincial income taxes or business taxes.
- Workmen's Compensation
- Past due rent

I remember looking at a business that got into trouble and the lender had to sell the *security* to get paid back. At the time, the government was owed $200,000 in payroll deductions. The first $200,000 that the bank collected from the sale of *inventory* and collection of amounts owed to the business had to be given to the government. Each lender deals with a *margined operating loan* a bit differently so make sure you understand how yours works.

All definitions will be included in your offer letter and you will need to submit a *"margin report"* either monthly or quarterly depending on what you negotiate with the bank. You need to understand what you can include in your margin and what is considered a *priority claim*.

How To Impress Your Banker

Managing Accounts Receivable

You want to make the most of your business and manage it the best way possible. That includes making sure your customer is good for any amount you sell them and allow them time to pay you and that you do get paid. Things to consider about managing your *accounts receivable*:

Make some enquiries about clients before you let them charge purchases. Depending on where you live, you can do a *business credit report*, and your banker can ask for a *bankers' report* without the consent of the business. Your banker will know whether that is the case where you live. The *business credit report* will tell you where your client gets credit and what their payment history is. The *bankers' report* will tell you things like whether there is an *operating loan*, the average balances used, the average cash balances, and if there has been a cheque returned NSF (not sufficient funds). Tell your banker what you do to qualify someone for an account. When I knew a borrower checked out his customers before giving them an account, I knew the *accounts receivable* had a higher chance of being collected. If a borrower is simply giving customers an account in order to increase sales, the chances they won't pay are much higher.

Follow invoices to make sure your clients pay. Once the due date is reached, make a follow-up phone call. Clients sometimes forget, or if they are short of cash, they'll pay the squeaky wheel before the silent one. You might get paid and someone else might not. By collecting your receivables before ninety days, you can show your banker that your collection processes are good.

Understand your industry. You might provide a client thirty days to pay but sometimes the larger clients might not pay for 90 or 120 days. You know they are good for it but that is how they do business. Explain that to your banker and see if you can't get an exception to include that amount as an *eligible account receivable*. Give them a good reason—the company's great payment history, for instance, or the fact that it is publicly traded or rated.

Export Development Corporation (EDC) has a program that insures up to ninety percent of some foreign receivables for a fee. If you are an exporter and see some risk in being paid, see what EDC can do for you. You can normally borrow more against an insured receivable and often up to ninety percent. On a $10,000 receivable that is insured, you will be able to borrow $9,000 rather than the usual 75%.

Lenders will consider other things, such as the number of customers you have and whether one is very large when determining how much they will lend you based on the *accounts receivable* you have.

Managing Inventory

Inventory depends on the type of business. Things to consider about managing your *inventory*:

If you are a retailer or wholesaler, you will have only *finished goods* as *inventory* so the margin amount will be a set percentage of the value of the *inventory* you have.

If you are a manufacturer, you will have a much more complicated margining formula. *Raw materials*, *work in progress,* and *finished goods* will be margined at different percentages. *Finished goods* are ready for sale and are considered to have the highest value so will normally be margined at the same value as the *inventory* of a retailer or wholesalers. *Raw materials* and *work in progress* will depend on their marketability. Most lenders give no value to *work in progress* and may provide some value to *raw materials*. If your *raw materials* are a commodity like oil, then a higher value is given to it.

In a margining formula, *inventory* is reduced by

any potential claims the supplier might have. If, for instance, you go out of business, a supplier can take back the *inventory* within thirty days, which means the lender cannot sell it to pay back your loans. Have a discussion with your lender to understand what potential claims might be and which apply to your *inventory*.

Managing Accounts Payable

Managing *accounts payable* is equally important as it will affect your credit rating and the amount of time suppliers will give you to pay them. Things to consider about managing your *accounts payable*:

Take a two percent discount if you can afford it. In the long run, it will save you money.

When we had the store, some suppliers gave us a discount if we paid early. It's a fairly standard practice that's referred to as "2%10/net 30". That means we got a two percent discount if we paid in ten days but paid the full amount if we didn't pay for thirty days. While early payment increases the length of the *cash cycle* because you pay earlier, in ten days instead of thirty, and you perhaps use your *operating loan* more and for longer, you can still save a lot of money. As an example, if we bought $100,000 of *inventory* from a supplier and paid for it in ten days, we only had to pay $98,000 but if we didn't pay until thirty days were up we had to pay the full $100,000. We could save $2,000 if we paid early. Compare that to the interest we might pay on an *operating loan* for $100,000 for the twenty extra days which at five percent equals less than $300 ($100,000 x 5 percent x 20/365 days). If we paid late, there was often a penalty of around two percent, which meant instead of paying $100,000 we had to pay $102,000. Understand the terms your supplier provides and the cost-benefit of paying earlier if you are given a discount.

If you are not offered a discount to pay early, take the entire time, say thirty days to pay. You have the use of someone else's money for that time so it costs you nothing. You conserve cash and don't have to use your *operating loan*.

Pay on time, whatever your supplier is offering. If you don't, there could be a cost associated with late payment, as in a late payment fee. Worst case, your supplier will make you pay for your purchases when they are delivered—often called cash on delivery—and your credit rating will suffer.

Managing Your Operating Accounts

Managing your operating accounts carefully—*accounts receivable* (the amounts you are owed), *inventory,* and *accounts payable* (what you owe suppliers) can save you money and more importantly, helps to build your reputation with your banker and your customers, whether they be purchasers of your *inventory* or suppliers.

Term Loans or Leasing

Term loans are used to purchase equipment, finance *leasehold improvements,* or in some cases finance *owner-occupied real estate*. Leasing is simply another form of financing.

Equipment Loans

Term loans for the purchase of equipment are scheduled to pay back the entire amount over the life of the equipment. If you purchase machinery for $100,000 and you expect it to last five years, you can likely borrow up to 75% of the cost of the machinery or $75,000. The repayment schedule will combine principal and interest payments to make sure the $75,000 plus interest is paid off over five years. As part of the deal, you need to maintain the equipment and keep it insured.

Leasing will finance up to 100 percent of the cost of equipment plus delivery and installation costs so it can conserve your cash. The leasing company retains ownership of the asset but any warranties will be transferred to you. You can purchase the equipment back at the end of the lease for the estimated fair market value only if you exercise the buy-out option. You don't have to. You can simply give it back.

In many cases, leasing is preferable, particularly if the equipment might be obsolete at the end of the lease. If you still plan to use it, however, you can purchase it. In addition, sometimes leasing can save you taxes as you may be able to deduct the entire amount of your lease payments from your income. Check that out with your accountant.

Many banks will provide what is referred to as a pre-approved *equipment loan*, whether by way of loan or lease. If you need to acquire equipment that can often be the way to go. The offer letter will describe what you can finance with the loan and the percentage. If the piece of equipment fits the description of what is okay to finance, you can access the pre-approved loan.

Let's take a look at how a pre-approved loan works.

You get a pre-approved loan for $150,000.

You borrow 75% for one piece of equipment that costs $100,000 so the loan balance is $75,000 and you have $75,000 available.

Over the next six months, you pay back $30,000, which means you now have $105,000 available and the loan you took out has been reduced to $45,000.

You want to buy a piece of equipment for $140,000 that fits the definition of what you can borrow for. You borrow $105,000 or 75% of its value by using what's left in your pre-approved loan.

As you pay down the loan, the amount is freed up for another purchase. It can save you time as you don't need to reapply. You simply need to advise the bank and they will most likely take *security* on the piece of equipment you just purchased.

Equipment loans can have either fixed or variable interest rates but leases are generally fixed rates. A variable rate loan follows the prime rate and will change with the direction of the prime rate. For fixed-rate loans, the payment does not change for the term of the fixed-rate (you can usually choose 1, 3 or 5 years) and for a lease line, the payment amount does not change for the life of the lease.

Leasehold Improvements

When you start a small business or move into a new location, you will likely need to make some changes to the interior—like moving walls or installing shelves. The landlord may finance that as part of the lease payments but if not, you might need to get a loan. While you are renting the premises, you own these *leasehold improvements* but once you move out the ownership of the *leasehold improvements* transfers to the landlord. In order to protect themselves, lenders will likely only finance leaseholds over the term of the lease so the loan will be paid off before the lease expires. If you decide to move at the end of the lease, the landlord becomes the owner of the *leasehold improvements* and if the loan is not paid off, you will have to continue to make payments on it.

Leasehold improvement loans can have either fixed interest rates or variable.

Owner Occupied Real Estate

Normally, when we think of real estate, we think of mortgages. However, when you buy real estate to house your own business it will, in most cases, be financed with a *term loan*. It is the success of your business that pays the loan back and the bank relies on that.

Mortgages, on the other hand, are most often only for investment properties. The value of the building, as well as the payments on the mortgage, will come from the rents that are paid by the companies leasing the units.

Government Sponsored Loans

Years ago, the son-in-law of one of our clients opened a new retail shop and needed $150,000 for *leasehold improvements*. We offered him a government-guaranteed loan. The father-in-law thought the administrative fee of $3,000 charged by the government to *guarantee* the loan was too high, so we made the loan and replaced the government *guarantee* with his *personal guarantee*. When the retail store closed its doors and went out of business, our client tried to negotiate his way out of the $150,000 *guarantee* he had provided but he couldn't make that happen. What seemed like a good idea at the time cost him $147,000.

Under the *Canada Small Business Loans Act,* the Government of Canada will guarantee certain types of loans for small businesses including those to purchase or up-date commercial buildings, purchase new or used equipment or invest in *leasehold improvements*. Under the *Canadian Agricultural Loans Act*, the Government of Canada will guarantee the loans of individual farmers and farm products marketing co-operatives and in Quebec, *La Financiere agricole Du Quebec* will provide loans to farmers or forestry operators. Canada Small Business Loans charge an administrative fee and the other government-guaranteed loans limit the interest rates charged and the *security* provided.

The maximum amounts and terms and *conditions* of these government-guaranteed loans change frequently but your banker will know the details at the time. You need to weigh the costs and benefits before you decide to proceed with the *guarantee* or not.

Letters of Credit or Letters of Guarantee

A *letter of credit or a letter of guarantee* can be issued on your behalf by your banker. It means that the bank "guarantees" that payment will be made. For example, if you are a start-up business or doing business internationally and are not known to your buyer, your customer might require a *letter of credit* to make sure they will be paid. You pay a small percentage of the amount of the *letter of credit* to have it issued (say 2%) and perhaps a small fee (say $100) to the bank. However, if the bank has to make payment on the *letter of credit*, the amount that is paid out becomes a loan to you and must be repaid. Usually, it becomes part of the *operating loan*. If you pay the invoice on receipt the *letter of credit* expires.

Remember that once a *letter of credit* is issued, it is normally irrevocable which means if the party it is issued to asks for payment, they will be paid whether or not they have lived up to their end of the deal. It is like a certified cheque. You can protect yourself by having your bank issue a documentary *letter of credit* that outlines the documents that have to be presented before a payment is made.

Other Offerings

Conventional lenders offer some more complicated products that can be used for specific purposes. We'll look at a couple of them.

Derivatives

A foreign exchange *derivative* loan helps you manage the risks of dealing in other currencies and provides some degree of certainty in your cash flow. If you are an exporter or order equipment from another country, unless you can have the price set in Canadian dollars, likely the value of the Canadian dollar will not be the same when you get paid or have to pay for equipment. You can buy another currency to be delivered at a date in the future when you expect to receive or spend funds and lock in the cost. You know in advance how much you will receive or have to spend in Canadian dollars.

You can also buy an option on foreign exchange which provides you with a choice of whether to buy the currency at that rate in the future or not. It costs you money upfront but you can decide to use it or not depending on what happens with the currency.

Similar products exist for interest rates, which allow you to fix rates on a variable loan and pay floating rates on a fixed-rate loan or buy an option to do so. The product is normally called an interest rate swap loan—you can "swap" a fixed or floating to the other one.

Derivative loans for currency or interest rates should only be used to provide certainty to your cash flow. The limit is set by the bank and is considered to be part of your overall loans. Your offer letter may even indicate that you can only use the loan for the operation of your business not to speculate on foreign currencies or interest rates.

Asset-Based Lending (ABL)

Another form of an *operating loan* is an *asset-based loan*. It works the same except the lending limits are usually higher and it is much more expensive. The lender hires (but you pay) a third party to come into your business and give a value to the assets you have given as *security*. The value is provided as a "net orderly liquidation value" or the amount the bank could get if it sold the assets in a specified amount of time—not a fire sale. The third-party provides a report and updates it at least annually or however often is specified in your agreement with the bank. Depending on what it is asked to do, the review may include how you manage your *inventory* and collect your *accounts receivable* and how accurate and efficient your in-house reporting systems are. All of this may give the lender sufficient comfort to increase the margin amount of your *inventory* and *accounts receivable* and provide you with a larger loan.

One of our clients had an ABL that had daily reporting of the value of *inventory* we were using as *security*. It was very expensive for them, but the *inventory* was a commodity so current pricing was immediately available and the third party report indicated the *inventory* control systems were extremely accurate. We were able to lend 95% of the value of *inventory*. In a non-ABL situation, we probably could have only margined at 50% of that value. The bottom line for the client was that while it cost them to do the daily reporting, they were able to borrow almost twice as much on the same *inventory* and because they needed the cash, it was worth it.

An ABL is not for everyone. Because it is so expensive, it usually doesn't make sense unless overall *operating loans* are in excess of $5 to $7 million. Keep it in mind though if you are growing and need more cash than a non-ABL *operating loan* provide.

Offers to Finance

There are those who live by the rule "better to ask forgiveness than permission," but I wouldn't advise adopting that attitude if you want to make friends with your banker. Over my twenty years as a banker, I asked only two small business owners to find another bank. Both were very profitable and ran a good business. The only problem was they refused to live up to the commitments in their contract with the bank. At some point, I knew they would hit the wall and someone would have to pick up the pieces. It was a long time coming, but one of the companies was bought out in 2006 by a publicly-traded company that had negative cash flow. The other still seems to be operating although it is still private and its *financial statements* are not available. Time will tell.

Once you have negotiated financing, the bank will put the terms and *conditions* in a contract that you both sign. This is referred to as an offer letter. The contracts vary in their name—an offer letter, a commitment letter, an offer to finance to name a few—but they are all contracts. The bank agrees to lend you money in return for your agreement to meet the terms and *conditions* of the contract.

Most loans to small businesses in Canada are *demand loans* and most offers include clauses like "loans are repayable on demand" and "availability is at the sole discretion of the bank." The demand feature of loans is not something that is fully understood by either bankers or clients. A demand loan is just what it sounds like. The bank can refuse to increase your loan even though you are not at your limit and paying as agreed or can ask you to repay any outstanding loans. It doesn't matter whether the interest rate is variable or fixed. The bank does not have to give a reason as long as they give you adequate notice (as defined by laws where you do business). While non-payment is the usual reason, there can be others. In my first job as a banker, we asked a limousine company to repay our loans as the business had expanded to include activities that were not permitted under our policies and perhaps may even have been illegal. We gave no reason and were paid out by another bank.

The offer letter includes the entire agreement between you and the bank. Make sure your banker explains what everything means and what you are committing to. If you don't understand, ask. Much of what causes grief between a banker and a client is simply a misunderstanding or lack of communication. You and the bank need to trust one another. That means you need to understand what is expected of you and stick to your commitments.

These are the main points in any offer letter:

The details of any facilities you have with the bank including amounts, interest rates and fees and repayment.

Use for intended purpose: Make sure you use each loan solely for the intended purpose. If you have an *operating loan*, use it to fund day-to-day operations, like *timing differences*, and long *term debt* for capital expenditures. Match the repayment period of your loan to the life of the asset.

Interest: Once your business is established and profitable, as your business grows you may be offered interest rates on Canadian loans based on B/As (*Bankers' Acceptances*) or U.S. dollar loans based on *LIBOR (*London Interbank Offer Rate). These are the rates that banks charge each other for short-term loans and it is a lot less than you pay. You borrow the money at the same rate as the bank does and it guarantees repayment of the loan. In return, you pay them a s*tamping fee.* Your overall cost of borrowing including interest and the *stamping fee* is much less than your cost of prime-based or fixed-rate loans.

Security: The letter will name the *security* you have provided for the loans. For most borrowers, the owners, and perhaps others will *guarantee* the debt personally. Before you get the loan, you'll sign a form referred to as a *Guarantee and Postponement of Claim*. The guarantee means that you commit to pay back any loans made to the company if and when you are asked to. It is not necessary for the bank to sell any *security* it has from the company before it sues you. It can sue you at the same time and collect from whoever has the money. The *Postponement* part of the form is often overlooked and ignored if it is not properly explained. It means that if you lend money to the company, you will not pay any of it back without asking the bank and getting written permission. It is referred to as a postponed shareholder loan. Remember, it is considered *equity* in your company and can affect your pricing.

Life Insurance: One of the standard features of *security* is life insurance on any individual that is considered critical to the operation of a business. As an owner, that may well be you. Have your banker explain it to you. If you do not have life insurance on your loans and have guaranteed them, the bank can ask your estate to pay loans back. If you have life insurance, the life insurance company does that.

Covenants. Positive *covenants* are things you have to do and negative *covenants* are those that you agree not to do. Some offer letters include financial *covenants* as part of their positive or negative *covenants* and some have them separate. Reporting *covenants* are what you agree to provide the bank and may be separate or intermingled in positive *covenants*. Whatever they are called, make sure you understand them and comply with them. How to calculate financial *covenants* varies and you need to follow the formulas provided in your offer letter. While most loans are demand, not living up to the terms of your contract is a good reason for a bank to ask you to repay them.

Conditions Precedent. Some offer letters will outline things that you need to do or documents you have to provide before you can use your loan. As an example, *conditions precedent* to most loans are that you provide a signed copy of the offer to finance and the *security* is registered.

Jurisdiction. Each *jurisdiction* has a set of laws and your agreement will be governed by the laws in existence in the *jurisdiction* outlined in your offer to finance.

Acceptance. Make sure you accept the offer before the drop-dead date that will be noted likely at the end of the document. If you sign it after the acceptance date it becomes null and void.

Schedules. Most offer letters have schedules attached. These include any definitions that are required and any reports you have to fill in and submit. For example, if you have a *margined operating loan*, a schedule will be attached to your offer letter that you need to fill out to determine the amount available.

$$$$$$$

Every loan is unique as it should be tailored to meet your individual needs and your company's needs. This chapter has shed some light on some of the common features of different kinds of lending facilities to give you some insight into "bankspeak." I will reiterate that the relationship with your banker should be considered a partnership. I often tell my students that if a customer will not communicate with you before loans are approved, it is highly unlikely it will happen after the money flows. Most importantly, you need to understand what you commit to in return for that money. If you don't, simply ask.

In the next chapter, we'll look at alternate forms of financing—those that are not considered "conventional" and may be of interest to some folks.

Chapter 6

Non-Conventional Sources of Financing and What They Mean

Chapter 5 detailed the kind of loans that are provided by banks, what I call *conventional financing*. Here, we'll talk about some of the more common *non-conventional financing* types: *angel investors, venture capital, mezzanine,* and *subordinate debt, Business Development Corporation* and *equity* financing. While a detailed description of all types of *non-conventional financing* and how to go about accessing them is beyond the scope of this book, it is important for you to understand the terminology and concepts of some of the most common types. This chapter will explain the major differences between *venture* or *angel* capital, *mezzanine debt*, *subordinated debt,* and *grants.* In some cases, some sources of cash are described in more than one of the sections. And finally, a head's up: you'll need to make sure you fully understand the contract you are signing and what it means to both you and the other person putting in the cash. We'll explore when your company might qualify for the different types of cash and where the type of *non-conventional financing* falls in the *waterfall* of payments. It focuses on the less established businesses—not only pre-commercialization businesses but those that are smaller and need *capital*.

Non-conventional financing is just that. It comes in many different sizes and shapes and is in addition to services provided by private-sector financial institutions, as *BDC* calls them, or *conventional financing* as I refer to them. This chapter provides a summary of the most prevalent of them and the concepts you should understand in order to make your conversation with any lender bear fruit.

But, before we go into the details on those, it's important to understand there are basically only two sources of cash for a company—debt or *equity*—and they are very different animals. You need to understand more about how banks and investors look at the two sources of cash or types of financing.

On the conventional side, there's **debt**: a lender provides loans and is paid interest based on the amount of the loan and the risk that it might not be paid back. The downside to the lender is the amount of the loan and what it costs to collect it. The upside is the interest they earn on the amount borrowed.

Equity, on the other hand, represents ownership in the company. An investor provides cash to the company to purchases shares. The downside for the investor is (just as it is for a lender) that he or she can lose the whole amount of the cash if the company is not successful. The upside is limited only by the success of the company. The more successful a company is, the more the shares are worth.

We spoke in an earlier chapter about guarantees. If your company is incorporated, you are one of the shareholders and perhaps the only one if you own the entire company. With smaller companies, lenders usually require the shareholders to personally *guarantee* loans, which means the shareholders have to pay back loans if the company cannot. This backstops the risk to the lenders and transfers the risk to the shareholders. If you have limited resources available to pay back the loans if the company fails, a lender may require someone to co-sign the loan, meaning the co-signer agrees to be as responsible to pay it back as the borrower is. If the company does not succeed, that co-signing can ruin relationships.

For example, let's assume your company needs $100,000. If the lender lends you that the amount and is paid interest at 5%, the best case is the $100,000 gets paid back and the lender earns 5% on the $100,000 or $5,000 a year. The worst case is the money is not paid back and the lender writes off all or part of the $100,000 and pays all of the costs associated with trying to collect as much as possible. If the $100,000 is invested as *equity*, the downside is the same for the equity investor as the lender—up to the entire

$100,000 might not be returned if the company fails.

That's the downside. On the upside, an equity investor gets paid by a share of the *profits* and the increase in the value of the shares purchased. If the investor pays $100,000 for fifty percent of the company and the company is successful, the equity investor is entitled to share in fifty percent of the *profits*. So, if the company makes $100,000 in profit, the equity investor is entitled to $50,000. The amount may not be paid until some time in the future when the shareholders agree that the company has sufficient cash to pay it. In addition, if the value of the shares increases, their investment is worth even more. Quite a difference between what the conventional lender gets as a return and what the equity investor gets for the same amount of money! If you ever hear the comment that a lender is not paid enough to take *equity* risk, it means that a lender is limited to the interest on the loan but an equity investor can make a lot more money than that.

There are many variations in the ways that companies handle repaying their investors, whether it's straightforward debt or *equity*. It all depends on what is agreed to between the parties and what works best under the circumstances. I call it a *waterfall* of payments—the order, or priority of payments the company makes to those it owes money. At the top of the *waterfall*, there's debt—that gets paid first. At the bottom is *equity*. It gets paid last.

Let's use the money you borrowed to buy your home as an example of a *waterfall*. If you paid $400,000 for the house and the bank lends you seventy-five percent of that amount, it will take a mortgage on your house for $300,000 and you agree to a repayment schedule. As long as you meet the repayment schedule, you can continue to live in the house. However, if you stop paying your mortgage payments, the bank has the right to ask you to move out, *foreclose* on your house, and sell it. If your mortgage has paid down to $275,000 and the house sells for $300,000, the bank will get the first $275,000 plus the amount it cost them to sell the house and you will get what's left. If the house sells for $250,000, the bank gets all of that and, depending on where you live, can sue you for the rest of the money. The *waterfall* is pretty clear—the bank gets paid first and you get paid last.

When a company is operating, day-to-day bills are paid as they are due. Scheduled payments like interest on loans and any principal payments (debt repayment) are made based on the agreements made between the parties. Typically, all debt is paid back before *equity* can be withdrawn, or there is a limit to the amount of money a shareholder of the company can take out.

If the company is no longer operating and closes its doors, the *waterfall* will define who gets paid first from the cash generated from the sale of assets of the company. If the company has conventional debt, the banks are at the top of the *waterfall*. The shareholders are at the bottom—they get paid if there is anything leftover at the end.

Angel Investors and Venture Capital

I met with my good friends Wendy and Corey Keith at El Cortez Mexican Kitchen and Tequila Bar in Edmonton. We sat outside on metal chairs at tables that were glazed with ceramics and very colourful, apropos for a Mexican restaurant. The sun was just setting behind the trees and it was a magnificent late summer evening.

Corey is the president of Keith and Associates. He and I met in 1994 when I moved to the credit approval department at the Royal Bank of Canada (RBC) in Alberta. I was immediately dubbed the "expert" in Knowledge-Based Industries (KBI). It was then a new type of financing that every financial institution in the market was trying to corner. I suspect I got the portfolio as no one else wanted it. Corey was an account manager in Saskatoon at the time and a trailblazer and pioneer in KBI. It didn't take us long to link up at the first KBI conference, and we have been friends ever since.

Corey worked with RBC and *Business Development Bank of Canada* (*BDC*) and developed relationships and business contacts both in the finance industry and KBI. In 2002, he decided to hang out his own shingle and Wendy joined him in 2004. He and his associates work with both start-ups and established companies. I have lent to start-up businesses but have not been personally involved with *venture capitalists* or *angel investors*, so I turned to Corey for information.

Corey is like the George Foreman of financing. The companies that Corey works with span the entire market: from people with great ideas with no business structure or financing to established businesses that need advice and want to go public. He helps those just beginning (what we call "pre-commercialization businesses") get the start-up money—*grant*s or *equity*—to develop the idea enough for them to get *conventional financing*.

Corey explained to me that he helps clients understand when the various kinds of financing make sense and how to access them. Why and when people need money varies widely and ranges from helping them get a new idea off the ground to helping finance a product or service that's already in demand. The risks and types of money available are almost as varied as the ideas themselves.

Venture capital is a term that pops up a lot—partly because it's often used to describe *angel investing* as well. Corey tells me that 99.9% of small businesses will never qualify for *venture capital*. I told him about being surprised to learn that even many conventional lenders had not heard of *angel investors* and did not know the difference between the two. Corey nodded and smiled and was not the least bit surprised. He explained that the two types of investment are markedly different.

Venture capital is typically higher dollar amounts, in the ten-million-plus range, with set investment objectives such as a set return on investment. Most *venture capital* investors are passive and do not get involved in the day-to-day management of the business. Many invest their money in a *venture capital* fund, whose manager makes the decisions on what companies to invest in, and investors simply sit back and wait for their share of *profits*. The funds invest in a pool of companies and buy shares (often referred to as taking an ownership) in each of them.

Anyone that has watched the *Dragon's Den* sees a different kind of *Venture capital* at work. The five dragons pick the companies they will invest in and, based on what they are prepared to invest, negotiate what percentage of the business they want in return. The person or persons providing the money does not typically get involved in the decision-making. Although *venture capital* companies often take a position on the Board of Directors of the company they invest in as a way to protect their investment. The decisions are based on how successful they think the company can be and the return they can expect—high growth, high return.

Angel investing shares many of the same principles as *venture capital*, but on a much smaller scale. It also is rare for most small businesses but more accessible than *venture capital*. The dollar amount is less and the angel is prepared to invest time (generally at no cost) and money in the right management team. *Angel investors* don't just bring money to the table, they also bring along the business acumen and contacts that the small business owner might not otherwise have.

According to Mike Volker (an *angel investor* and *entrepreneur* in Vancouver) in his *Globe and Mail* article in October 2017, "More than 600 companies attracted $3.2 billion in *venture capital* last year—the most since 2001. In comparison, angels invested in thousands of companies." Most small businesses don't qualify for either but if you can find an angel that is a good thing. If your business gets to the point where *venture capital* is an option, you need to seek professional advice.

Corey introduced me by email to one of his associates, Fred, who is an *angel investor*. I had my conversations with Fred on the telephone although I did a google search to see what he looked like. He was very open, with a great sense of humour, and helped me understand his philosophy in investing in companies as an angel. He is from a fairly small town in Alberta and helps make companies work.

I learned a lot in my discussions with Fred and one of the most important takeaways for me was that the way an *angel investor* provides money and gets paid is flexible and based on "the deal that two people can strike." The approach is not a cookie-cutter one, unlike *venture capital* which usually has set investment criteria and specified returns. Fred has put money in a company either by buying shares or providing a loan, depending on the situation, and each is properly documented to ensure everyone knows how the deal will work. "Good paper makes for good friends," Fred says.

As an example, a few years back a friend and client of Fred's who owned a company died. Fred arranged for three individuals to each buy one-quarter of the company, and the widow kept a quarter. He was very specific in his choices of investors—the brother-in-law of the widow to make sure that everything was above board, an employee, who was committed to the business and "coachable," and Fred himself. Two years later, the employee bought them all out and is now the owner of a successful business. There was no pre-set price for the buyout but the four owners haggled out an agreement. Each investor made a good return on their investment, the business thrived, and the employee became the owner. Everyone won.

Fred is now seventy years old. Over the years, he

has invested in sixteen different companies that range from start-ups to established businesses. He still has investments in two and was on his way to meet with one of those when we spoke. He limits his investing to locations where he can be hands-on—and to people who are "coachable." His theory of investing seems straightforward "much rather an A team with a B product than a B team with an A product." In short, Fred invests in people. Over the years, he has focused his investments in businesses where the individual is the "major horsepower" behind the business and is not afraid to learn and grow with the help of a mentor. His investments have ranged from $25,000 to $200,000; he lost money on only three of the sixteen.

The length of time Fred will leave his money in the company is flexible and subject to events. He has invested in some companies for as long as ten years. He does sometimes include a repayment date. Other times, circumstances dictate the repayment. He has never been involved with a company that went public, so he has always been repaid by the business owners.

As an *angel,* he sometimes gets in disagreements with other shareholders. He once put money in a company and while he wasn't specific about the disagreement it couldn't be resolved through negotiation. Instead, the company went to auction and the shareholders bid on it. He was paid out when one shareholder bought out the others.

Fred never actively solicited investments and many were brought to him through his business as a Chartered Accountant (now a *Chartered Professional Accountant*) or referrals from friends. He quickly acknowledged that that was before the rules changed. Before that, there were no conflict of interest guidelines, but when they were introduced he could no longer invest in his clients. I was naïve enough to ask him what he expected potential companies to provide and was surprised to learn that he did not ask for *business plans*—he called that "government speak" or "bankspeak." Because he invests in people, he explains, he provides the business acumen and they bring the "attitude." That attitude is displaying the willingness to work with a mentor, ask questions, and learn.

I asked Fred if there were companies he would not invest in. He does not invest with people that have a bad credit history so like the banks he relies on *character*—one of the five *"Cs"* of credit. He believes that if individuals are irresponsible with their own money, they will be irresponsible with his. Family stability is a plus, in that it allows individuals to focus on the business. He also wants them to have some money in the game. If he is the primary investor, he looks for control of the business, or fifty-one percent ownership. How long he retains controlling ownership will depend completely on how the investment goes.

He sometimes will back off of control if the individual proves himself, and sometimes he keeps control until he is paid out. It depends. He avoids investing in companies where the owners know everything and just want money, or as he puts it "just give me the money and let me run." He finds this attitude is prevalent with inventor types and has steered clear of that type of investment. He finds technology companies have more surprises and tends to avoid them as well. He wasn't specific about surprises but in my history of dealing with technology companies, there are a lot more unknowns, like bugs in computer software, that can make the company go off the rails. One of his write-offs was a technology company; the other two were simply because, as he put it, he "backed the wrong horse."

Fred tells me that the earliest *angel investors* are family and friends. While I've certainly known of many family or friend investors, I had never thought of them that way. These familiar angels may not add much in the way of mentoring but are there because they have faith in the individual. This is not a bad thing and can certainly help a person ... but as I have mentioned earlier in the book, it is a sad statistic that most new businesses fail, and when friends and family lose money in the endeavour it can change relationships dramatically. The trouble, quite often, is that family and friends invest because they believe in the concept but do very little due diligence. They just want to help out.

Corey tells me that *angel investors* usually fall into four different camps:

Non-Industry Investor: Typically a non-industry investor does not have the industry know-how to mentor the owners. They may simply be looking to diversify and are looking for a good return.

Industry Investor: The industry investor may have worked, or is still working, in the industry and will often play a role as a mentor as well as financier.

Regional Investor: The regional investor invests only in projects in their region or community. They simply want to "give back" to their community and may be less focused on return. I would classify Fred as a regional investor.

Supplier/Producer Investor: This type of investor invests in companies that purchase their product or service to benefit their own business.

If your company is a candidate for an *angel investor* or *venture capital*, do your homework and understand what each individual or fund is focussed on. Concentrate your efforts on those that match what you have to offer.

Mezzanine Financing and Subordinated Debt

Mezzanine financing is a hybrid between debt and *equity*. *Mezzanine debt* can simply be a loan or it might include a kicker. A kicker lets the investor buy the company's shares at some point in the future.

Small companies need cash to survive. If you don't have enough and can't find investors, your company might try and get some *mezzanine debt*. Your idea is great but not proven enough for sufficient *conventional financing* or *equity investors*. While *mezzanine debt* is "subordinate" to *conventional financing*, in the *waterfall* it comes behind them but before *equity*. Mezzanine financers often have an option to get a percentage ownership at some point in the future and have a seat on your Board of Directors. The terms of the share option are negotiated into the contract and potentially provide a further upside if the company is successful. *Mezzanine debt* holders vary in size from established banks to smaller investors.

All *mezzanine debt* is subordinated but not all *subordinated debt* is *mezzanine debt*. *Subordinated debt* simply means debt that comes after conventional debt and before *equity* in the *waterfall*. *Angel investors, venture capitalists,* and *mezzanine* financiers that put money into a company in the form of a loan fall into the category of *subordinated debt*. This means they only get paid if there is enough money after *conventional financing* is repaid. But, because it is in the form of a loan, they get paid before the shareholders do.

So, in my *waterfall*, your banker would be paid first, the *mezzanine* cash provider second, and you as the shareholder last. *Subordinated debt* has no *equity* component. You simply negotiate with the *subordinated debt* holder that repayment will not take place before certain terms and *conditions* are fulfilled and usually that relates to repayment of the conventional debt first. If *angels, venture capitalists,* or *mezzanine debt* holders put money into a company in the form of *equity* they are not considered to be *subordinated debt*, but rather *equity*. They are even further down the *waterfall*, at the very bottom—they only get paid back if there is any money left after everyone else has been paid. If a company can't make it day-to-day, it is highly unlikely that anyone, even the conventional lenders will be paid off in full.

Both mezzanine financing and *subordinated debt* get paid a higher rate of interest than conventional debt, as their risk of not getting paid back is higher. These types of investors will scrutinize your management team and past cash flow results to assess the level of risk in lending to you. If your company is not successful, they will be paid back only after the conventional lender is, and in most cases, they don't get paid back everything they are owed. They need to rely on you and your past performance. In essence, they're betting on your likelihood of success.

Business Development Bank of Canada (BDC)

There was a time when *BDC* was considered a complementary lender to conventional lenders; it still claims to complement the role played by private-sector financial institutions but that is changing somewhat. As in the past, they do not provide *operating loans* but still provide cash to operate to companies and take *security* behind (or *subordinate*) to the conventional lender. *BDC* will provide loans to purchase assets, real estate, and companies. They generally have less stringent policies than a conventional lender as their only mandate is to help small business and they don't have to worry as much about regulations and shareholder returns. They even sponsor the CBC program the *Dragon's Den*. You might want to meet with one of their folks to see if they can help you. Keep in mind though, more is not always better. Always remember that you are expected to pay back whatever you borrow.

They advertise themselves as the bank for *entrepreneurs* (not personal loans) and specialize in a range of products from financing start-ups to established companies. *BDC* is a Crown Corporation but operates independently from its only shareholder, the Government of Canada. It provides financing, *venture capital* investing, and consulting services to small businesses. If your company cannot borrow what is needed from a conventional lender and you need some advice, *BDC* might be able to top up what you need.

BDC does not take deposits or provide *operating loans*. They will, however, provide an *operating loan* subordinate to a conventional lender's, and give an *entrepreneur* what they call a working capital loan. As part of the negotiation, they will specify how much the conventional lender can collect in the *waterfall* before they get money. If you qualify, *BDC* and your bank will work together to provide your company with the amount you require. I can recall negotiating with a company and *BDC* to provide operating capital. Between the three of us, we agreed that we would give them an operating line of up to $500,000. If the company wasn't successful up to the $500,000, we came first in the *waterfall*. We could take the first $500,000 collected and pay off loans. However, any amount collected over that amount would pay down *BDC*. If we lent the company $600,000, the last $100,000 wouldn't have been repaid until after *BDC* was. All this may not make a difference to you, but your lender and *BDC* will want you to understand. In that case, *BDC* was subordinate to my bank for up to $500,000 but the rest, if there was any, was not.

Grants

Grants are set up to back any number of initiatives. Your banker can give you some advice on *grants* in your area or you can contact your local Chamber of Commerce. Some companies, such as Keith and Associates, will apply for *grants* on your behalf and do all of the research for you. *Grants* are neither debt nor *equity* but can be an important source of cash for your company. As long as you meet the terms of the *grant*, you won't have to pay the money back.

Non-Conventional Financing

As we said in the beginning, *non-conventional financing* is just that. The only common thread is it falls behind *conventional financing* in the *waterfall* of payments. You need to ensure you understand exactly what you are signing and agreeing to. Make sure all the details are explained to you.

Chapter 7

Niel and Valley Floors Inc.—A Case Study

The meeting took place in a boardroom, and I took a seat to the side so the direct conversation could be with the bankers and my client. I chatted with Damian, a director on the bank's small business side, while we waited for the other two to join the meeting— Krista was the relationship manager at the bank and Niel who had taken a phone call. While he was out of the room, I explained to Damian that I had met Niel a couple of years before and why it was so important that we get him set up with a line of credit and get his company established with a bank.

The bankers were dressed in business casual clothes—Damian in a suit with an open-necked shirt and Krista in a skirt and blouse. Niel was dressed in his work clothes. He had on his green tee-shirt and you could see the tattoo of Liz on his arm. He had on work pants which were covered in what you would expect—paint, glue, and dust. He wore the tools of his trade on his belt and pulled out what must have been a foot and a half long screwdriver and laid it on the table in front of him. There was no doubt he had left his place of business to come to this one.

Within days of the meeting, Niel had a $30,000 operating line of credit and a $20,000 Mastercard, with an autopay, to help him manage his cash. Let's look at the process and how we got there.

I introduced Niel in Chapter 1 and have provided glimpses of him throughout the book. He is in the flooring business and installed cork throughout our condominium when we did renovations—it ended up being about 2,300 square feet. Calgary is very arid and some of the seams in the cork widened to the point that I was afraid I might fall into some of the ruts. Although our contractor went out of business and we had no receipts, Niel made things right. He came back on his own time and his own dime and fixed the things that weren't working with his initial install. Niel takes his business seriously and believes it is the outward manifestation of his *character*. He is proud of what he does and that is clear in his integrity. Standing behind his word is part of him.

Once I got to know Niel, I asked him if he was interested in telling his story through my book. That was in the early stages when I had just started to write it and while I had a vision, I wasn't sure how his story would fit in. I did know and explained to him that he would have to share information that up to now had not been public, and he was okay with that. I knew, though, that he was exactly the kind of small business person that needed to understand "bankspeak" and I felt I could help him.

Niel represents the essence of what Statistics Canada calls microbusiness—those that have less than four employees. They are for the most part hard workers and very skilled at their trade but unsure of the banking system—if, and if so how, it can help them and their businesses. Like many microbusiness owners, I knew that Niel could benefit by understanding "bankspeak" and what value having a good relationship with a financial institution brings. Niel was pleased, as many small owners are, that someone outside his direct circle would take an interest in his business.

Niel told me he relied on a credit card to bridge the gap between what he had to buy and when he got paid for it. He isn't alone. Michael, a small business person before he joined the bank, took one of my courses, where I teach bankers how to lend money to small and medium-size businesses. He made a point that I had not thought of—small business folks rely on credit cards because it is easy and that's all they know. They are happy to have the flexibility and don't even think of the cost. They are just happy to have credit readily available without having to face the daunting visit to a bank.

In the early days in February, Niel and I discussed how an *operating loan* together with a credit card could save him and his company money and help those who worked with him get paid every two weeks rather than the thirty days he had to wait for his invoices to be paid. He was very interested. As is often the case with these discussions, we both got busy and didn't communicate for months. Then, out of the blue, the first week in November, I got a text message from him that said "I think I'm ready for that line of credit. Also my company is about to double in size. Exciting times." I had to travel to Vancouver the next day so agreed to meet the next week over dinner.

In the interim, we texted about the amount of loans he felt he needed and came up with a range between $25,000 and $50,000. I needed to know that before I contacted a lender to set up a meeting.

During dinner, we learned his business had changed. When Niel worked on our renovations, he bid on the flooring through one of his suppliers and hired someone to do the tiling in the shower stall and bathtub. His girlfriend Liz (they are now married) used to help out in her spare time but just after our renovations finished she moved to another city to study music. She now lives there and has a contract to teach music for a couple of years. They commute every second weekend or so. He works six days a week and takes Sundays off.

Niel now works for a large residential landlord in the city and it makes up about eighty percent of his business. The relationship started with him being a one-man show, contracting to do flooring for two suites a week. Because of his workmanship and work ethics, he was asked to bid on all the work needed in recently vacated apartments to make them suitable for the next tenant. That included flooring, painting, plumbing, and baseboards. He was now a general contractor and hiring others to do what he was not licensed to do (more about that later). The result was an initial doubling of his business and a significant need for cash. I learned that for years he had been running his close to $200,000 a year business by way of a Mastercard with a limit of only $10,000. Although he was clearly a master at managing his cash, clients didn't pay on a schedule that allowed him to pay off the amount he charged on the card every month so it always carried a balance. He knew it cost him a lot with a 19.9% interest but like most small businesses, he didn't know what else was out there. He now realized that the credit card was insufficient to meet his, and his contractors' needs, and he needed to explore other sources of cash. Our journey started and we got to test my theory that most small businesses had the ability to get a loan from the banks if only they knew how to prepare and were able to talk to them in terms both understood.

Niel told my partner and me that he had started using accounting software, Quickbooks, about a year before and it helped him better understand where he was making money. A lot of the jobs he thought were great were actually costing him money. He had changed his pricing and as he put it, "I am not here to get money I don't earn, but I do deserve to be paid for what I do." He does not have a contract with his new customer, but he bids on jobs and gets paid a set amount for a job based on a unit factor. For example, he gets paid a fixed rate to lay a square foot of flooring so he knows going in what he will be paid. He asked upfront if reputation played a role in their decision to hire him as a contractor and they acknowledged it was a major factor.

It is quite a different beast to deal with such a large business and Niel has learned through his mistakes what he should and shouldn't do. For example, he learned an expensive lesson when he did not get paid for work that the superintendent onsite told him needed doing. He now only does work when he has a signed purchase order.

Niel and I had previously chatted about his personal *credit score*. He told me he had worked really hard to get a solid credit rating. Before he came to Alberta, he didn't pay much attention to it but when he got here he realized how important it was. That speaks to the first "C" of credit that we outlined—*character*.

Up to now, we had only talked about "big picture" things so I needed to get his *financial statements* and make my own assessment of the company. Luckily enough, he had accountant-prepared tax returns that included a *balance sheet* and an *income statement* as well as personal *financial statements* and tax returns for him and Liz. Sales ranged from a low of about $165,000 in the last year to a high of about $210,000 the year before. Quickbooks had obviously helped as his profit margin after paying himself went from less than one percent to twenty-five percent. Last year, Niel also bit the bullet and bought a new truck for the business. That year, even with his new truck, debt service was over six times. Recall that means he generates enough cash after expenses to pay his scheduled debt repayments and interest payments six times over. (Although the calculations vary, I used earnings before interest and taxes (*EBITDA*) divided by principal plus interest payments).

I asked Niel what bank he wanted to deal with to apply for the credit line he badly needed. Once he decided, I phoned my friend Judy who worked in a different department and she gave me Damian's name. As a Director in the small business side, he could help point me in the right direction. I phoned him and when I started to explain my background he reminded me he attended a couple of training courses I had done for the bank a few years before. It is indeed a small world.

I told Damian that my client was a small business that had been around since 2008 and moved to

Calgary in 2011 when it incorporated. In my opinion, the company needed a line of credit, and Niel was now ready to apply. When I explained the debt service of the company based on his last year was over six times, Damian was quite impressed. I asked him what was needed from us before we met. He explained at the level of loans we were looking for a lot of the decision was based on personal credit history. Damian introduced me by email to Krista, the Relationship Manager, and sent a personal statement of affairs that Niel and Liz needed to fill out. After I asked Niel's permission, I shared his name and the name of the company with the bank.

Liz and Niel came to dinner in late November and I gave them the personal statement of affairs to fill in. They passed it on to Damian and Krista and based on Niel's schedule we arranged a meeting with the bank the next week which was the first week of December. I reinforced to Niel that it was his meeting and he needed to be prepared to answer any questions they might have. I was simply there to provide back-up if it was needed.

The day of the meeting, Niel answered a few questions I had on his *financial statements* before we headed to meet with Damian and Krista. The only two pieces of advice I had to give him for the meeting were to be himself and reinforce that he was not reliant on the residential landlord as his only source of income.

It is always a good news/bad news story when a small business has a highly successful customer as the only client. As long as relations are good, all is well. However, if things go wrong there is no longer a revenue stream.

Still wearing his work clothes, Niel drove me in his truck and of course we went to the wrong place first. The bank had a large branch close to where we were to meet and we went there by mistake. We eventually ended up at the right place and were met at the door by Damian.

The meeting lasted almost two hours and the bankers spent the time getting to know Niel and Valley Floors better. The questions were about his beliefs and how he conducted business. The financial performance of the company hardly drew a question.

Niel did stress that while eighty percent of his revenue stream was now with the residential landlord, he maintained his association with two general contractors who called him if they had work. He was not relying on one source of income. Damian made the point that you need to stick to your core competency but be able to read your market and be adaptable.

Niel explained that Valley Floors was a licensed flooring contractor and had also hired an apprentice to train and help him out. He said, "If you want folks to view contractors differently, you have to carry the message." His message was that whatever work you do, it has to be done right, regardless of whom the tenants are and whether they are owners or renters. He was asked how he protected himself from shoddy work by the sub-trades (as I had asked him) and he was very clear. He only hired licensed, bonded, and insured sub-trades. He carried insurance through Western General Insurance and as long as he was true to who he hired, the insurance would cover him. According to Niel, that is public knowledge within the industry.

Damian made the point that Niel must be very good at managing cash to have succeeded this long on so little, but it was time that he took my advice and applied for a line of credit (also known as an operating line). Niel pointed out that over the years he had promised his sub-contractors that he would take care of them, and all they had was his word. He simply said, "Take a chance on me and I will feed your kids. I will pay you when I can but it may be thirty days." He had made the point to me in earlier discussions, and again to the bankers, that in order to pay his sub-trades, he had eaten peanut butter and crackers for days on end as that was all he could afford. He continues to hire only licensed, bonded, and insured sub-trades so his insurance covers his company for any shoddy work they may do.

Niel gets paid by the residential landlords within thirty days of the time a suite is inspected and those terms are included on the purchase order. He needs an operating line so he can pay his sub-trades every two weeks and his suppliers within the fifteen-day terms they offer. He is billing about $55,000 every thirty days so he needs about $30,000 before he receives payment on his invoices.

Niel told the bankers that he believed in marketing Valley Floors and he relied on a piece of advice in *Rich Dad, Poor Dad*, a 1997 book by Robert Kiyosaki and Sharon Lechter. He said that attending marketing and sales seminars had a big impact on his success to date. He has learned, and firmly believes, in using the company name, Valley Floors, whenever he is speaking to someone so they have the name embedded in their heads. They recognize it when they hear it, unlike the names of most of his competitors.

The meeting ended very cordially and both sides stressed the need for transparency and building a long-term relationship. Niel has lofty goals and wants to continue to grow and, based on the meeting, it seemed the lenders wanted to share that success with him and to help him along the way.

We left with a promise to receive an email with any further information that was needed the next day. Krista asked if I could be included in the email and Niel acknowledged that he considered my partner Jack and I friends and mentors so that wasn't a problem. True to their word, the next day we received a request for two years of financial information for Valley Floors and a personal tax return for Niel for the previous year. With Niel's permission, I scanned them to Krista immediately as he was on-site working.

Krista continued to communicate with us by email to advise us of timelines and when we could expect to receive a proposal of what they were thinking. The formal "Expression of Interest" was received on the following Monday. I have seen my share of these and there was nothing in it that I didn't expect except I thought the pricing was a bit high. However, I did recall the discussion with the bankers that they would provide the best pricing they could with the initial deal as it bordered on immoral to reduce the rate because somebody complained or had a competing offer. The cost was still a lot less than the 19.9% Niel was paying on his credit card balances and he was fine with it. The Expression of Interest detailed the things Niel needed to know and he told me that he agreed with what was in it. The facilities being proposed were what we asked for—a $30,000 line of credit and a $20,000 credit card. The "Expression of Interest" also included prices and terms and *conditions* including *security* (a *General Security Agreement* covering all assets of Valley Floors Inc., a personal *guarantee* from Niel for $50,000, and "any other *security* that… [the bank and/or its solicitors]…reasonably consider necessary in the circumstances"). In an Expression of Interest, the bank usually will leave room to add anything in the final deal that was missed initially or felt needed to protect its interests. It is simply an outline of what the lender is comfortable in recommending to the folks that have to approve it and it is often called a discussion paper, but it is not an offer to finance. What most borrowers don't understand is that the person they speak to cannot approve the loan—they only influence what is approved. Any information you can give them only aids the process and helps them better explain your business and needs to the folks that ultimately approve the loan.

I had a few questions about how the proposed pricing and fees worked so I emailed Krista to confirm that my understanding was correct. I needed to know that the fee for the line of credit included automatic revolving (funds would be placed in the account as needed and taken out when there was excess cash) and we could establish the credit card on an autopay system (the balance was taken from the current account and any shortfall would be funded with any amount that was not being used on the line of credit). The autopay meant that Niel didn't have to keep track of the payment date on the credit card. The date the balance on the credit card was due the bank would take money out of the banking account and if there wasn't enough it would be paid by the line of credit he had established. That made sure that no interest was paid at the higher rate charged on the credit card if there was money in the bank account or if he hadn't fully used the line of credit that was at a lower rate.

Once Krista confirmed my understanding, Niel and I had a conversation and, the same day, he told Krista to go ahead as he was happy with the Expression of Interest. Niel was going to Dublin for a wedding and Christmas and needed to manage his business long distance. He needed approval of the credit line and credit card, as well as a fully functioning electronic banking within eight days. A big order for sure.

The lender approved Niel's request the next day, he signed on the dotted line two days later, and everything was operational before he left for Dublin.

From the first visit to Niel's chosen lender until he was signed up was a mere eight days. Within another four he was operational and able to use electronic banking to manage his business from outside of the country. That's pretty impressive in my opinion and goes to show how simple the process can be.

Niel's story is an example of how important the first "C" of credit is—*character*. I get it that as a company gets larger the other "Cs" (*collateral*, *conditions*, *capacity*, and *capital*) come to play. Had Niel not had a good track record personally and worked at improving his *credit score* I can almost guarantee he would not have had his request approved so quickly with the bank, and perhaps not at all. It reinforces that *character* is the first hurdle and if you can't pass that one, the other four "Cs" become a moot point. It didn't hurt that Niel very honestly and effectively conveyed his *character* and who he was in the meeting with the lenders.

Six weeks after we first visited the bank, I texted Niel to see how things were going and he said, "[The bank] is going wonderfully and I couldn't be happier." His work with the residential landlord would pick up again in February and in the meantime, he had managed to pick up two large jobs through his other contacts so he has kept busy. It showed once again that not having all your eggs in one basket is a good thing. Niel was able to pick up jobs when his primary contract temporarily slowed down. A good news story for sure.

We had Niel up for dinner not long ago, and he expressed something I never thought of. Just because you have the money doesn't mean you can take your eye off the ball of your operations. Niel did for a while but now is back on track.

Our next adventure was to meet with a couple that wants to start a brewpub. My partner has a specialty in location analysis and market research and that together with the financial advice I can provide should set them in the right direction. We'll see how that goes. The financing required will likely be a lot more than Niel needed so the other four "Cs" will come into play as will the other elements of "bankspeak."

Glossary

A

Accounts payable: What a purchaser owes suppliers for goods or services they provided.

Account(s) receivable: What a purchaser owes a vendor for goods or services sold to them. Once the purchaser is billed, the amount owing is called an *account receivable*.

Adjusted EBITDA: *EBITDA* stands for earnings before interest, taxes, *depreciation* and *amortization*. Each person that lends money may define Adjusted *EBITDA* a bit differently. It is meant to calculate just how much cash is available to pay back principal and interest on loans. An example is the amount of cash calculated by *EBITDA*, less additional costs including taxes, dividends to shareholders and whatever the company paid for *fixed assets* that it did not finance.

Aged listing of accounts receivable: A dated record of the bills a company sends to clients. Your bank may ask for this to help them understand how quickly customers pay and whether or not they can rely on your collection of those receivables to pay back their loans.

Angel investor: Somebody who will invest time and

money in a business and its owner. An angel brings money as well as knowledge and contacts to a business.

Asset-based lending: A type of loan that relies heavily on the value of the assets that secure it and is usually based on *inventory*. It is an expensive way to finance as it relies on outside audits to value the *security* as well as the company's technological ability to report, but it may be worthwhile as a source of cash.

B

Balance sheet: Shows what a company owns (assets) and the source of the money that was used to buy them (liabilities and owners' equity).

Bank of Canada Rate of Interest: The overnight rate at which major financial institutions borrow and lend one-day (or "overnight") funds among themselves; the Bank of Canada sets a target level for that rate and announces it on eight fixed dates during the year. Usually, when it changes, the *Prime Rate of Interest* will change.

Bankers' Acceptances: Often referred to as B/As, these are only available as Canadian dollar loans. (See *LIBOR*, London Interbank Offer Rate, loans for information about the equivalent in other currencies.) B/As are a secure and often a less expensive way to borrow money. The bank guarantees it will pay back the lender if the company can't, and the company borrows at the same interest rate as its lender would, which is typically lower than the company would pay. While the bank charges a fee (called a *stamping fee*) for these loans, the all-in cost is still less than if the company were to borrow without the bank's *guarantee*.

Bankers' report: A report from your client's bank that summarizes the client's business accounts. It will tell you things like whether there is an *operating loan*, the average balances used, the average cash balances in the account, and if there has been a cheque returned NSF (not sufficient funds). You would ask your bank to do a Banker's report for a new client to make sure they can pay you what they owe and have a history of meeting commitments.

Billing cycle: This is the time between bills. The billing cycle with credit cards is normally monthly so the billing cycle will be from 28 days (February in a non-leap year) to 31 days depending on the number of days in a month.

Business credit report: These are supplied by credit reporting agencies. The report outlines a business's payment history and how much credit it has and where.

Business Development Corporation (BDC): The BDC is a crown corporation owned by the Government of Canada. It lends money and provides advice to small businesses and describes itself as being "dedicated exclusively to *entrepreneurs*."

Business plan: This is where a company sells itself and its idea. The plan outlines how the company will repay potential lenders, including what it will do to generate sales, why it will be successful (noting details on why folks would buy from this company instead of the competition), as well as the particular skills of its owner and employees. The plan also names the basis of the research and sources used to make the assessment. Above all, a *business plan* needs to be realistic and based on facts.

C

Cs of Credit: There are typically five "Cs" of Credit that a lender considers when assessing a loan. They are *character*, *collateral*, *conditions*, *capacity* and *capital*.

Canadian Agricultural Loans Act (CALA): Aimed at increasing the availability of loans to farmers and agricultural co-operatives, the *CALA* states that the Government of Canada will guarantee loans made by banks as long as the loans are made within its rules and regulations.

Canada Small Business Loans Act: Aimed at increasing the availability of loans for small businesses. The Government of Canada will guarantee loans made by banks as long as the loans are made within its rules and regulations. These loans are called Canada Small Business Loans.

Capacity: The amount of cash available to invest in the business, from the owners personally or elsewhere if things don't turn out as planned.

Capital: Also referred to as *equity* or owners' equity, *capital* refers to how much money the owners have in the business, whether it is cash used to buy shares (*share capital*), or the *profits* not paid out of the business as dividends (*retained earnings*).

Cash cycle: The average time it takes a company to buy, make, and sell a product and collect what people owe for it.

Character: Who the owners and the borrower are. Basically boils down to how the individual and owner have dealt with debt in the past and why someone should trust that they will repay loans.

Chartered Professional Accountant (CPA): An individual who has met the professional standards required to become an accountant.

Collateral: What a borrower provides to a lender to sell if the business is not successful. It is considered a second way out of the debt.

Conditions: What a borrower agrees to do or not do in return for the lender trusting them to repay shareholders' or depositors' money. *Conditions* are included in the contract referred to as an Offer to

Finance.

Conditions precedent: Actions a borrower needs to take or documents it needs to provide before the company can use the loan.

Conventional financing: A term I use to describe what banks provide. The most common are *operating loans* (also called revolving lines of credit) and *term loans*.

Contingent liability: Something that the company may have to pay in the future. Examples are letters of credit or letters of guarantees or a lawsuit that is pending but not yet finalized.

Corporation: A legal organization that limits the liability of the shareholders. Although it costs more to establish a *corporation* than a *sole proprietorship* or *partnership*, doing business under an incorporated company has some advantages:

- •A *corporation* is a legal entity and the shareholders simply own shares. Whether they are involved in management or not, the shareholders invest in the company and are not otherwise responsible for what the company does.

- •Owners who are also employees of the company will be treated like any other employee. Note that salaries to owners are taxed differently than dividends, so you need to get professional advice on which is the most appropriate for you as an owner.

- A *corporation* continues to exist until it is shut down by the shareholders who own the shares at the time. The ownership of the shares can change hands and the *corporation* will continue.

In Canada, there is only one form of *corporation*, but in the U.S. there are three.

Cost of goods sold: The amount it cost to buy or make what the company sold.

Covenants: Outline what the company agrees to do, and not do, in exchange for the money the lenders are prepared to lend to it. *Covenants* are contained in the Offer to Finance.

Credit Bureau: Provides the credit reports that provide a *credit score*. There are two types:

- *Hard credit bureau*: Shows what a borrower's *credit score* will be if a requested loan is approved.

- *Soft credit bureau:* A "what if" scenario that shows what a borrower's *credit score* is before a requested loan is added to their debt.

Credit score: An assessment of how well the owner manages personal finances taking into account how much is owed, and to whom, whether payment terms are met, and how often credit is applied for. Your *credit score* has a big impact when you are looking for a loan for your company, as lenders feel business debt will be handled the same way personal debt is. The score ranges from 300 to 900; higher is better. The more debt the owner has and the more often he or she applies for debt, the lower the *credit score* will be.

Crowdfunding: A concept where people go online and ask for money. It is not a "loan" because it does not have to be paid back, and it is not a grant as it does not have any *conditions* attached. It is simply folks who want to help out by giving money. Not reliable as an ongoing source of cash.

Current assets: Assets that will provide cash within a year. Most common are *accounts receivable* and *inventory*. *Current assets* can also include things like prepaid expenses such as rent that is paid in advance.

Current liabilities: Money that needs to be paid within a year. *Current liabilities* include things like trade payables to pay for *inventory* that was bought and the amount of debt that needs to be paid within a year.

Current portion of long-term debt: The amount of term debt that must be paid in the current year.

Current ratio: Reveals how able a company is to pay its current bills when they are due. The standard formula is *current assets* divided by *current liabilities*, which include what the company owes on debt in the upcoming year.

D

Debt service coverage ratio: How many dollars are available to pay what is owed to the bank and any other lender each year (principal plus interest). Typically calculated as *EBITDA* or *Adjusted EBITDA* (as defined by your lender) divided by principal and interest that is owed over the next year.

Default: Means the company has not lived up to the terms and *conditions* of the agreement that was signed in order for the bank to lend it money.

Demand loans: The type of loan that allows the lender to decide on a minute-by-minute basis if they will lend the company money or not. It is their money and they can decide. Most small business loans, unless they are government-guaranteed, are *demand loans*.

Depreciation and amortization: Represents the wear and tear on a fixed asset as it is used. While it is a non-cash amount (the company paid for the asset when it was bought) it represents how much of that asset was "used" during the period in question.

Derivative: *Merriam-Webster* defines this term as "a contract or *security* that derives its value from that of an underlying asset (as another *security*) or from the value of a rate (as of interest or currency exchange) or index of asset value (as a stock index)." In a banking context, a *derivative* is a way for a company to lock in interest or currency rates for a fixed period. For example:

If a company purchases a piece of equipment for a future delivery date and the price is in U.S. dollars, it can "lock in" the rate it will pay for the U.S. dollars when the equipment is delivered. This provides certainty about the cost of the equipment.

If a company has loans with floating rates of interest and thinks that interest rates will go up, it can swap its floating rate and pay a fixed rate instead.

E

EBITDA: Earnings before interest, taxes, *depreciation*, and *amortization*. It, or a variation of it, is often used to determine the dollars available to pay what is owed the bank each year in order to determine the *Debt Service Coverage Ratio*.

Eligible accounts receivable: *Accounts receivable* that a bank considers to be good and which they will lend money against.

Entrepreneur: In my mind, *entrepreneurs* are business people who keep trying. If something doesn't work, they pick themselves up, dust themselves off, and try something else.

Equipment loans: *Term loans* for the purchase of equipment. Principal and interest are set so that the entire amount of the loan, plus interest, is paid back over a period of time that does not exceed the life of the equipment.

Equity: Tells you how much money you have in the company in *share capital* or *retained earnings*. Sometimes called Owners Equity.

F

Financial statements: Generally come in three levels: Audited, Review Engagement, and Notice to Reader or Compiled. Depending on the level of statement, you might have different information but you will always have a *balance sheet* and an *income statement*. *Financial statements* are the responsibility of management. In summary:

•Audited financial statements: Have been verified by an independent auditor (usually a *Chartered Professional Accountant*). The auditor provides an opinion and "reasonable assurance" that the *financial statements* are free of material misstatements and are in accordance with generally accepted accounting standards. Audited statements are the only *financial statements* that provide an opinion.

—A "clean" or "unqualified" opinion means the statements are fine;

—A qualified opinion points out where

the statements are not in accordance with generally accepted accounting standards;

—An "adverse" opinion means the statements are not free of "material misstatements" or are not in accordance with generally accepted accounting standards; and

—A disclaimer of opinion means that the auditor will not express an opinion.

•*Review Engagement:* Completed by an independent accountant or bookkeeper, review engagements provide limited assurance that the statements conform to generally accepted accounting procedures.

•*Notice to Reader:* Cannot be guaranteed to have been prepared using generally accepted accounting principles. They are simply compiled from information provided by the company and no review of systems is conducted. I like to compare this to the company that takes its receipts to the accountant in a shoebox and asks the accountant to prepare *financial statements*.

Financing gap: The amount of money the company needs to cover the time between when it is paid and what it has to pay out in order to operate. It has to be paid either through cash or loans to the company from a bank or shareholders. The standard formula is *accounts receivable* plus *inventory*, less *accounts payable*.

Finished goods: What the company has produced and is ready for sale. One of the categories of *inventory* for manufacturers.

Fixed assets: The equipment and machinery used by the business, including manufacturing equipment to make the product, as well as office fixtures, such as desks and filing cabinets.

Foreclose: An act by a lender who took *security* on a loan to sell the *security* to pay back loans if the borrower cannot.

G

General partner: Manages a *partnership*. The *general partner* can commit the *partnership* and has unlimited liability for the obligations of the *partnership*.

General security agreement: Gives the bank the right to sell assets named in the agreement if the borrower cannot pay back the loan. The general security agreement includes personal property and does not generally include real estate.

Grants: A source of cash that generally does not have to be repaid provided the recipient lives up to the terms and *conditions* associated with the grant. Terms and *conditions* vary widely; it's important to understand what is being offered and what is expected.

Guarantee: A document the shareholder or someone else signs, agreeing that they will pay back the loans up to the amount of the *guarantee* (plus the associated costs) even if the company can't.

I

Income statement: Shows what happened to a business between year-ends. It includes how much revenue was generated and how much it cost to generate that revenue.

Industry risk rating: A financial institution's judgement of how risky a particular industry is. Each financial institution has its own rating scale.

Inventory: What it cost to buy or make what is sold. In most businesses, the *inventory* account is simply *finished goods* or what it cost to buy the *inventory*, but in a manufacturer's account, *inventory* is comprised of *raw materials*, work-in-progress, or *finished goods*.

J

Joint venture: A legal organization formed for the purposes of completing a project.

Each partner contributes either assets or management expertise (or a combination of both) to the *joint venture* in return for a share of the *profits*.

Partners pay taxes on their portion of any *profits*.

A *joint venture* ceases to exist when the project is completed and the assets and cash are distributed.

Jurisdiction: Outlines the laws that your company's loans will operate under and what laws will take effect if any legal action needs to be taken. The *jurisdiction* is included in the Offer to Finance that outlines the terms and *conditions* of the loan.

L

La Financiere agricole Du Quebec: An organization that supports the agriculture industry in Quebec and offers products such as insurance and financing support.

Land Titles Office: Place to register a lien on real estate. Mortgages are registered at the *Land Titles Office*.

Leasehold improvements: Any modifications made to premises leased by the company, like shelving or doors.

Letter of Credit or Letter of Guarantee: A promise issued by the lender to pay a set amount to a specified party if the company does not settle with the party. A letter of credit (or *guarantee*) is considered to be a *contingent liability*.

Leverage: The amount a company owes (liabilities) divided by *equity*. It measures how much others have invested in the company for every dollar the shareholders have.

LIBOR: London Interbank Offer Rate. These are loans in a currency other than Canadian dollars, most often U.S. dollars. B/As, defined earlier, are the equivalent of *LIBOR loans*, but in Canadian dollars. A *LIBOR loan* is often a less expensive way to borrow money as the bank guarantees they will pay back the lender if the company can't. The company borrows at the same interest rate as the bank would, which is typically lower than the company would pay. While the company pays a fee in addition to the interest rate the all-in cost is less than what the company would pay to borrow from a bank.

Limited liability partnership *(LLPs):* LLPs are similar to a *partnership* except that the individual partners are responsible only for things that they are directly involved with.

Law firms and accounting firms often organize as LLPs to ensure that if one lawyer or accountant is sued, the legal liability is limited to that individual, not the entire firm.

LLPs are quite common in all states of the U.S. but only some Canadian jurisdictions allow them.

Limited liability corporations (LLCs): LLCs are not

allowed in Canada but are common in the U.S.

LLCs are a hybrid between *partnerships* and corporations. LLCs are not incorporated but do limit the liability of the members, or shareholders.

Any income or losses are declared personally by the partners.

Limited partner(s): A partner who invests money in the business but is not actively involved in the management of the *partnership*. Similar to a shareholder in a *corporation*, a *limited partner* is only liable for the amount they invest. In rare instances, if it can be proven that the *limited partner* is actively involved in the management of the *partnership*, the *limited partner*s may be responsible for more than the amount invested.

Limited partnership: A *partnership* that has *general partners* and *limited partners*. *Limited partners* are treated differently than *general partners*, or the partners that operate the business. Refer to the definitions of both.

Liquidity: Does the company have enough cash to pay its bills on time? If so, it is considered liquid.

Long term assets: Assets paid for with money from the company that are not used in day-to-day operations. They can include things like investments in other companies or land that was purchased to expand the business in the future.

Long term liabilities: Anything that must be paid back over time. The amount of a loan required to be paid back in the current year is included in "*Current liabilities*" and is often called the *Current portion of long term debt*. The *long term liabilities* include the amount of the debt to be paid beyond that.

M

Margined operating loan: An *operating loan* that is approved for a maximum amount but the amount you can borrow is determined by the *margin report* you submit to the bank.

Margin report: A form that lenders require if a company has a *margined operating loan*. It includes an *aged listing of accounts receivable* plus *inventory*, and subtracts from that any "*priority claims*." For example, anything owed to the government is a priority claim. We all know that the government gets paid first.

Mezzanine debt: A type of *subordinated debt* that often incorporates both *preferred shares* and debt and always gets paid after conventional debt but before the common shareholders and the owner.

Micro-loans: Small loans, sometimes even less than $100, that are as diverse as the people lending the money. There are micro-loan companies that put lenders and borrowers together or lend money. There are also individuals who lend directly.

N

Non-conventional financing: Refers to any source of money other than what comes from a conventional lender (like a bank). This may include angel investment, *venture capital*, loans from the *Business Development Corporation*, government guarantees, and *grants*. It may also include *micro-loans* and *crowdfunding*.

O

Office of the Superintendent of Financial Institutions (OSFI): "An independent agency of the Government of Canada, established in 1987 to contribute to the safety and soundness of the Canadian financial system. OSFI supervises and regulates federally registered banks and insurers, trust and loan companies, as well as private pension plans subject to federal oversight."

Operating expenses: Selling, general and administrative expenses. The amount it costs to run the business, on top of what it costs to buy or make what is sold.

Operating loan(s): Used to finance day-to-day operations. It is another name for a *revolving line of credit* that is used when needed and paid down with any cash that's collected.

Overdraft: A loan facility where the bank agrees to pay cheques or debits to the account even if there is no money in it.

Owner-occupied real estate: The company owns the real estate where the business is operated.

P

Partnership(s): A business agreement where two or more individuals (known as partners) pool their talents and go into business together.

Similar to a *sole proprietorship* except that it has two or more partners who are fully responsible for any obligations of the *partnership*.

The partners are taxed personally on their share of the *profits* (or get a tax benefit for losses) whether or not they get paid.

The downside (or what to be aware of): Any partner can commit the *partnership* to obligations without the knowledge of the other partners, but every partner is on the hook for all commitments. Anyone dealing with any of the partners does not know what that *partnership* agreement says and has the legal right to take at face value what any of the partners say. In a proprietorship, the owner alone is the face of the business. In a *partnership*, each partner is responsible for any commitments other partners may make.

A *partnership* ceases to exist when any one of the partners exits the relationship. If any partner moves on or dies and the business continues to operate, it creates a new *partnership*.

Personal Property Security: Basically anything that is not real estate.

Postponement of Claim: A document signed by a lender other than the bank agreeing that they cannot receive any payment on their loan before the borrower gets written permission from the bank to do so.

Pre-approved equipment loan: A loan established for companies that purchase equipment on an ongoing basis. As long as the company purchases equipment that is approved by the lender when the loan is made, the company can pay for the equipment using the loan.

Preferred shares: A type of ownership in a company considered to be a combination of debt and *equity*. It is paid before the common shareholders and after the conventional debt.

Prime Rate of Interest: The basis for any variable interest loan announced by the lender whenever the Bank of Canada changes its overnight rate. All lenders tend to have the same Prime Interest Rate. A variable rate of interest will change any time the Prime Rate changes.

Priority claims: Any amounts of money that are legally required to be paid before the bank is paid.

Profit(s): Revenues less expenses.

Projections: The best assessment of how the company will perform in the future based on facts from market and industry research and a best guess of how the company may do.

Q

Quick ratio: Ability of a company to pay its current bills when they are due without selling any more of its *inventory*. The standard formula is calculated by subtracting the value of *inventory* from the value of the *current assets*, and then that result is divided by *current liabilities*. Current liabilities include the *current portion of long term debt*.

R

Raw materials: Items purchased in order to produce *finished goods*. Part of a manufacturer's *inventory*.

Retained earnings: The amount of *profit* left in the company after dividends have been paid out since the company was formed.

Revolving feature: Loans up to a specified lending limit that are automatically placed in the account if it is overdrawn, and excess cash taken out to pay down the loan.

Two-way revolvement puts money in the account if it is overdrawn and takes excess cash out of the account to pay down loans.

One-way revolvement just puts money in the account if it is overdrawn. It is up to the account owner to instruct the bank to make a payment when there is excess cash in the account.

Revolving line of credit: Another term used to describe an *operating loan*.

S

Security: What is given to the lender to sell if the loan cannot be repaid by cash generated by the company.

Share capital: The amount that shareholders paid for shares in a company.

Sole proprietorship: A single business owner, not separate from the business in legal terms.

The *sole proprietor* pays taxes on any *profits* from the business and is personally responsible for any losses or other obligations, such as paying for supplies or repaying a bank loan.

Anyone doing business with the proprietorship has the right to sue the proprietor, and the courts can force that individual to sell personal assets to settle the lawsuit.

The proprietorship ends when the proprietor chooses to end it or dies.

Solvency: If your company has more assets than liabilities, it is considered solvent.

Spread: The amount you pay for interest over the Prime Rate or USBR. If you are charged interest at Prime plus 2%, the *spread* is 2%.

Stamping fee: A fee you pay to the bank to guarantee that you will repay the money that is raised for your company on the public markets. It generally relates to raising money by way of Bankers' Acceptance or *LIBOR*.

Subject to financing clause: Means that a purchaser will buy either the business or the assets if he or she can get someone to lend them the money. It is not dissimilar to a *subject to financing clause* when you want to buy a house. You will buy the house if you can get a mortgage to fund it.

Subordinated debt: Paid after conventional debt and therefore considered to be "below" conventional debt in the *waterfall*, but above the shareholders. All *mezzanine debt* is *subordinated debt*.

Sustainable cash flow: The amount of cash flow your company can expect to generate without the effects of non-recurring events, such as the sale of an asset that is not used in the business or the purchase of a large amount of *inventory* that is on sale.

T

Term Loans: Loans that have scheduled repayments and are used to finance long-term assets such as equipment.

Timing difference: The time between when you have to pay for something and when you sell and collect the cash for it.

U

United States Base Rate (USBR): Equivalent to the Canadian Prime Rate; it is the base interest rate charged for U.S. dollar loans.

V

Venture capital/venture capitalist: A pool of *non-conventional* money and the people that manage it to help fund specific businesses. The money comes at a cost with high interest rates and the investors will most likely take an ownership in the company.

W

Waterfall: My way to describe the order in which money is paid. *Conventional financing* is almost always at the top of the *waterfall* and the owners are at the bottom. Other forms of unconventional debt are typically between the two and it is a negotiation between the parties to decide who comes first.

Work in progress: The amount of money that has been invested in manufacturing finished products.

ABOUT THE AUTHOR

Leslie D. Marion

I ended up in banking after graduating from Dalhousie University in Halifax in 1979 with a Master's Degree in Business Administration focusing on Finance and Accounting. In 1989, I became a Certified Management Accountant (now Chartered Professional Accountant, CMA). In 2016, I went back to King's College and received a Masters in Fine Arts in Creative Non-Fiction writing (2018), which planted the seed for this book. I could never understand the dichotomy that lenders didn't understand small business and vice versa. In **Easy Money**, I build a bridge with knowledge that will help both business and banks get what they need in the lending process.

In my over 40 years of banking—as account manager, risk manager and teacher—I have worked hard to make a difference to small businesses and in helping how lenders view their clients. I share the knowledge learned throughout this book.

There is a saying in the banking industry that if you have never made a bad loan, you have not taken enough risk. I can vouch that I have taken enough risk and did make some recommendations that ended up in loans being written off. Lending is a continuous learning process as no two loans are the same. I have also helped hundreds of lenders understand the psyche of small business owners and what they need to do to help make them successful.

When I left the bank to join my partner's business, I contracted my services to a big bank in Canada in the risk management department, concentrating on U.S.-based companies. Since 1999, I have taught in Canada and the U.S. and contracted to RMA out of Philadelphia, a major U.S. training company. I understand the similarities and differences between the Canadian and U.S. banking systems and regulations. In my capacity of consultant to RMA I have taken U.S. courses and converted them to the Canadian market, taught courses in the U.S. and taught U.S. courses in Canada with the help of classroom customization. The courses are developed to help lenders understand their customers better.

With this book, I think you'll find that both lending and borrowing money is an art, and a practice that transcends the Canada-U.S. border.